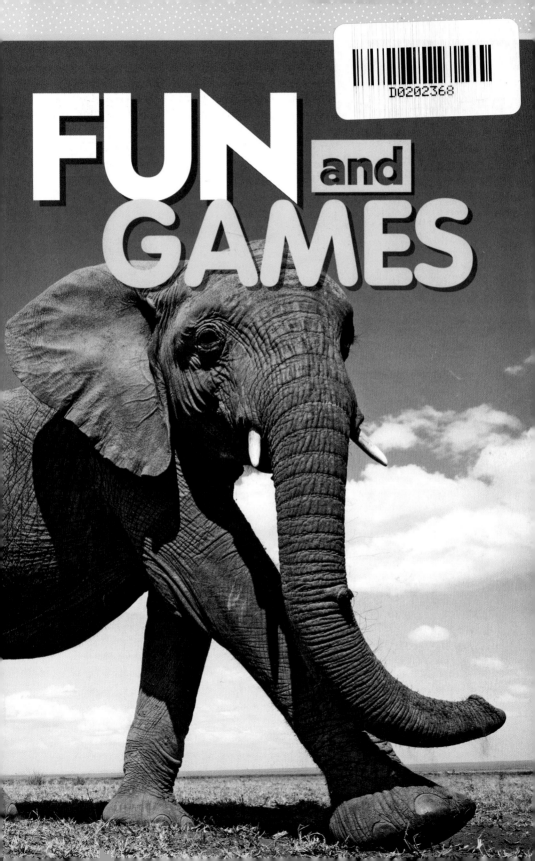

FUN and GAMES

WHAT IN THE WORLD?

BACK TO NATURE

These photographs are close-up and faraway views of different textures in nature. On a separate sheet of paper, unscramble the letters to identify what's in each picture.

ANSWERS ON PAGE 338

UDM

mud

WOTDSRNIFS

AAVL

Lava

SMSO

moss

NSESOT

LPMA AEFL

ERTE KTURN

REIEGCB

DSNA SUDEN

FIND THE HIDDEN ANIMALS

Animals often blend in with their environments for protection. Find the animals listed below in the photographs. Write the letter of the correct photo on a separate sheet of paper.

ANSWERS ON PAGE 338

1. spider	_____
2. frog	_____
3. bald eagle	_____
4. fox	_____
5. jaguar	_____
6. viscacha*	_____

HINT: A viscacha is a type of rodent that lives in South America.

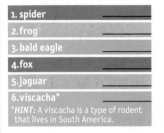

SIGNS OF THE TIMES

Seeing isn't always believing. Two of these funny signs are not real. Can you figure out which two are fake?

ANSWER ON PAGE 338

1. 212 Boring
2. SURFER X-ING
3. DUMP CLEAN DIRT HERE SEE 910
4. 45TH PARALLEL — HALFWAY BETWEEN THE EQUATOR AND THE NORTH POLE / PASS WITH CARE
5. W 37
6. NO NAME ST
7. SIGN NOT IN USE
8. SLIDE AREA
9. SMILE PLEASE

FUNNY FILL-IN

Ask a friend to give you words to fill in the blanks in this story and write them on a separate sheet of paper. Then read the story out loud and fill in the words for a laugh.

I was deep in the rain forest of __Joupon__ (country) with my friend __Aberham__ (famous person) searching for an ancient ruin called the Lost __Dump__ (noun) of the __Pigin__ (animal). But just __5,555__ (number) minutes into the journey, we realized we'd forgotten our __Beootle__ (type of insect) spray! A swarm of bugs were __Running__ (verb ending in -ing) us! We __Slowly__ (adverb ending in -ly) __Spring__ (past-tense verb) through the trees and soon smacked into a(n) __Bathamator__ (something hard). I pulled back some __Boysi__ (type of plant, plural) and couldn't believe my __Blue set__ (body part, plural). It was a part of the ruin—and we could hear __ding__ (sound ending in -ing) coming from inside! We peeked through a hole in the wall and saw a group of __Toys__ (animal, plural). They were lounging on stone __Black Bug__ (type of furniture, plural), snacking on __Salt cans__ (favorite food, plural), and even swimming in a pool filled with __Oringjuse__ (liquid). I guess this ruin isn't really lost at all!

Play more Funny Fill-In!
natgeokids.com/ffi

167

STUMP
YOUR PARENTS

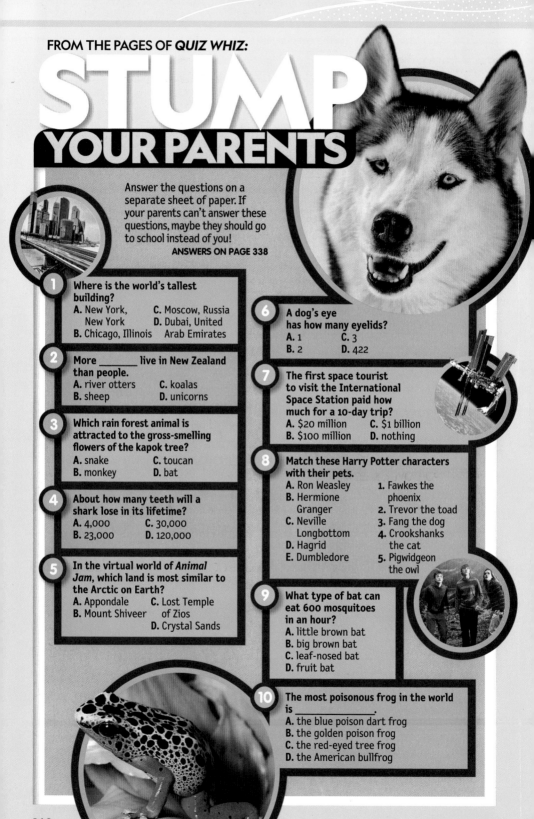

Answer the questions on a separate sheet of paper. If your parents can't answer these questions, maybe they should go to school instead of you!

ANSWERS ON PAGE 338

1 Where is the world's tallest building?
A. New York, New York
B. Chicago, Illinois
C. Moscow, Russia
D. Dubai, United Arab Emirates

2 More _____ live in New Zealand than people.
A. river otters
B. sheep
C. koalas
D. unicorns

3 Which rain forest animal is attracted to the gross-smelling flowers of the kapok tree?
A. snake
B. monkey
C. toucan
D. bat

4 About how many teeth will a shark lose in its lifetime?
A. 4,000
B. 23,000
C. 30,000
D. 120,000

5 In the virtual world of *Animal Jam*, which land is most similar to the Arctic on Earth?
A. Appondale
B. Mount Shiveer
C. Lost Temple of Zios
D. Crystal Sands

6 A dog's eye has how many eyelids?
A. 1
B. 2
C. 3
D. 422

7 The first space tourist to visit the International Space Station paid how much for a 10-day trip?
A. $20 million
B. $100 million
C. $1 billion
D. nothing

8 Match these Harry Potter characters with their pets.
A. Ron Weasley
B. Hermione Granger
C. Neville Longbottom
D. Hagrid
E. Dumbledore

1. Fawkes the phoenix
2. Trevor the toad
3. Fang the dog
4. Crookshanks the cat
5. Pigwidgeon the owl

9 What type of bat can eat 600 mosquitoes in an hour?
A. little brown bat
B. big brown bat
C. leaf-nosed bat
D. fruit bat

10 The most poisonous frog in the world is _____.
A. the blue poison dart frog
B. the golden poison frog
C. the red-eyed tree frog
D. the American bullfrog

LAUGH OUT LOUD

"JOEY AND TEDDY
LOVE MY NEW HOODIE."

"HE CAN ONLY FIND
SEVEN OF HIS SHOES."

"PULL OVER, SPEEDY."

"IF YOU DON'T STOP PLAYING POSSUM,
YOU'RE GOING TO MISS THE SCHOOL BUS!"

"YOU SAY YOU'VE BEEN FEELING
RATHER JUMPY LATELY?"

"I WISH YOU WOULD EAT LIKE OTHER SEA OTTERS."

WHAT IN THE WORLD?

TRUE BLUE

These photographs show close-up and faraway views of things that are blue. On a separate sheet of paper, unscramble the letters to identify what's in each picture. Feeling blue? **ANSWERS ON PAGE 338**

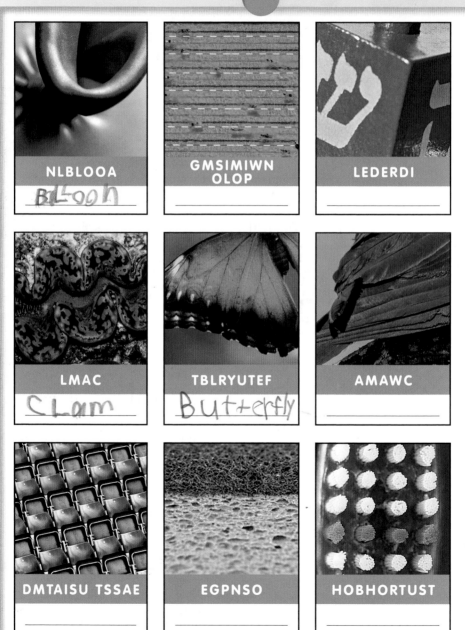

NLBLOOA

Balloon

GMSIMIWN OLOP

LEDERDI

LMAC

Clam

TBLRYUTEF

Butterfly

AMAWC

DMTAISU TSSAE

EGPNSO

HOBHORTUST

Just Joking

BLUE-WEBBED GLIDING FROG

KNOCK, KNOCK.
Who's there?
Cash.
Cash who?
No thanks.
I prefer peanuts.

Q How did **the lion** greet **the impala?**

A "Pleased to eat you!"

Q What do you call a shy lamb?

A Baaash-ful.

Q What protects a **clown** from the **sun?**

A The bozone layer.

171

ARE YOU A GARBAGE GENIUS?

How much do you know about trash? Take this quiz and write your answers on a separate sheet of paper, to find out if you're a waste whiz. **ANSWERS ON PAGE 338**

Hey! Don't throw away that doggie bag!

1 TRUE OR FALSE?

Before the days of trash collectors and dumps, people used to throw their trash on the streets for animals to eat.

3 PICK ONE

What makes up the bulk of waste around the world?
A. newspapers
B. plastic
C. food scraps
D. yard trimmings

4 FILL IN THE BLANK

Some _____ zip(s) around at 20 times the speed of sound.
A. garbage trucks
B. motorized trash cans
C. space trash
D. trash robots

5 PICK ONE

Which creepy crawlers can help compost your food?
A. crickets
B. centipedes
C. spiders
D. worms

Trash isn't just filthy— it's funny!

Here are some rubbish-themed riddles and jokes to try on your friends and family.

Q What has four wheels and flies?

A A garbage truck.

Q What did the waste collector say while digging through the trash?

A I'm down in the dumps today!

2 TRUE OR FALSE?

Old landfills are often turned into parks or green spaces.

THIS BOOK STINKS!

Check out this book!

FIND THE HIDDEN ANIMALS

Animals often blend in with their environments for protection. Find each animal listed below in one of the pictures. Write the letter of the correct picture next to each animal's name.

ANSWERS ON PAGE 338

1. sea star _____
2. crab _____
3. arctic hare _____
4. owl _____
5. antelope _____
6. chameleon _____

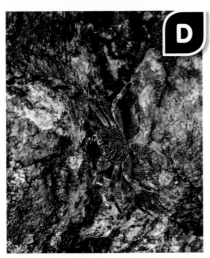

173

Ask a friend to give you words to fill in the blanks in this story and write them on a separate sheet of paper. Then read the story out loud and fill in the words for a laugh.

My band, the Three ___snakes___ (animal, plural), finally got our big break. ___Dimbey___ (male celebrity) was looking for kids to star in his new show, "___Vost___ (your hometown) 's Got Talent." We grabbed our musical ___sibs___ (noun, plural) and filed into the auditorium, where ___377___ (large number) people were waiting to audition. Finally it was my band's turn to perform. I took a(n) ___bomb___ (adjective) breath, then we started to play a rock 'n' ___flop___ (verb) tune. ___Dumb fool___ (relative's name) jammed on the ___run___ (adjective) keyboard and ___coner___ (friend's name) ___funping___ (past-tense verb) on the drums. Then it was time for my ___stiky___ (adjective) solo. I went to hit a(n) ___slimey___ (adjective) chord when my guitar flew out of my hands. I ___rubing___ (past-tense verb) backward and grabbed it in midair, but I lost my balance, crashed into the drum set, and broke the keyboard. I ___folrt___ (past-tense verb) off the stage and landed in the front row. Everyone was silent until ___Dumb___ (same celebrity) jumped to his feet and gave us a(n) ___funoph___ (verb ending in -ing) ovation. "___Judy___ (silly word)!" he yelled. "That was the best comedy routine I've seen so far. You're in!"

FROM THE PAGES OF *QUIZ WHIZ*:

STUMP
YOUR PARENTS

Answer the questions on a separate sheet of paper. If your parents can't answer these questions, maybe they should go to school instead of you!

ANSWERS ON PAGE 338

1 How many years can a macaw, a kind of parrot, live in the wild?
A. 5
B. 20
C. 60
D. 100

2 Each year, almost a million people travel to the Andes Mountains in Peru to see which cultural site?
A. Angkor Wat
B. Chichén Itzá
C. Machu Picchu
D. Stonehenge

3 Paper can be made from which of these materials?
A. panda droppings
B. hemp
C. wood
D. all of the above

4 A company developed what new kind of item after studying the way butterfly wings produce colors?
A. color screens for electronic devices
B. color-changing helmets
C. tie-dyed sunglasses
D. holiday lights

5 The tropical forest around the Lost Temple of Zios in the virtual world of *Animal Jam* would need long days and plenty of rain. If it were on Earth, where would it be found?
A. Arctic Circle
B. Equator
C. Great Barrier Reef
D. South Pole

6 On the Indonesian island of Komodo, which large animals do Komodo dragons eat?
A. water buffalo
B. blue whale
C. polar bear
D. hippopotamus

7 If you were to make a rain forest ice cream, which flavors could you use?
A. lemon
B. banana
C. mango
D. all of the above

8 Which type of animal is Rikki-Tikki-Tavi from *The Jungle Book*?
A. goat
B. bear
C. mongoose
D. meerkat

9 In the Sagano Forest in Japan, bamboo grows at a rate of _____ a day.
A. 1 inch
B. 12 inches
C. 40 inches
D. 60 inches

10 Spider monkeys have a prehensile tail, meaning they can _____ with their tails.
A. shoot venom
B. grab branches
C. peel bananas
D. scratch their backs

MOVIE MADNESS

It's chaos on this crazy movie set in Hollywood. Eleven things beginning with the letter *C* have gone missing. Find and write down on a separate sheet of paper the missing items in the scene so the show can go on.

ANSWERS ON PAGE 338

CRITTER CHAT

If wild animals used social media, what would they say? Follow this Galápagos tortoise's day as it updates its feed.

GALÁPAGOS TORTOISE

LIVES IN: Galápagos Islands, off the coast of Ecuador **SCREEN NAME:** SwellShell
FRIENDS:

TealToes
BLUE-FOOTED BOOBY

FrostyFur
HOARY BAT

LionAround
GALÁPAGOS SEA LION

START

11 a.m.

SwellShell
Boy, it's hot! Time to head up the "Tortoise Highway" to cooler ground for a few months. Thousands of tortoises made these tracks!

You weigh, what, 500 pounds? How fast can you cruise with that big backpack?
LionAround

SwellShell
My shell's actually pretty light—it's my legs that weigh so much! And it's not like I need to hustle to get food: I can go an entire year without eating or drinking.

A year's nothing to **SwellShell**—he's at *least* a hundred years older than me. Do you even remember your birthday?
FrostyFur

SwellShell
Nope! So I'll go ahead and celebrate today. Grass cake, anyone? 😊

2 p.m.

SwellShell
I feel like a mud bath. How's everyone else doing?

I'm feeling blue.
TealToes

Can I snag you a fish? That always cheers me up.
LionAround

No—it's a good thing! I'm going to flash these baby blues around the beach and try to get a date!
TealToes

Looking good, TealToes! Just like me when I get out of the water.
LionAround

6:30 p.m.

SwellShell
Sun's going down—time to find a patch of soil to snuggle down in. #PerfectDay

Are you kidding? It's party o'clock! Nighttime is when I can really spread my wings.
FrostyFur

Admit it—you come out at night for the bugs. And hey, I got plenty. I surround my nesting area with dung, so lots of flies over here!
TealToes

That's *fowl*. Get it? You're a bird—you're fowl. 😎
LionAround

177

WHAT IN THE WORLD?

SPACED OUT

These images show close-up and faraway views of things that are associated with outer space. Unscramble the letters to identify each picture. Seeing stars?

ANSWERS ON PAGE 338

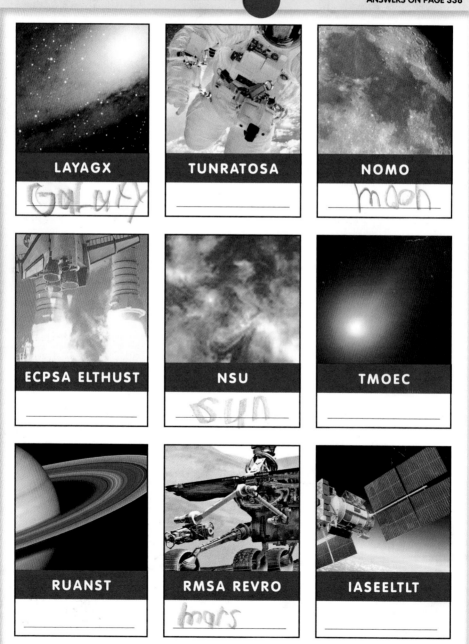

LAYAGX

Galaxy

TUNRATOSA

NOMO

moon

ECPSA ELTHUST

NSU

sun

TMOEC

RUANST

RMSA REVRO

mars

IASEELTLT

FUNNY FILL-IN

Ask a friend to give you words to fill in the blanks in this story and write them on a separate sheet of paper. Then read the story out loud and fill in the words for a laugh.

I've never been more _Dumpy_ (adjective). My baseball team, the _Green Bird_ (color) (noun, plural), was about to play the championship game. But Coach _Boging_ (celebrity) announced that the official rules had changed! First, every player would _Jump_ (verb) _99999_ (large number) times before going to bat. We also had to wear our gloves on our _But_ (body part, plural) like _Brows_ (article of clothing, plural) and run like a(n) _Puffin_ (animal). Before Coach could explain more, the umpire shouted, "_rip_ (verb) ball!" The umpire tossed me our new official bat, a(n) _drill_ (tool). When the _A Gamer_ (type of job) threw the new official ball, a(n) _rainbow_ (fruit), it zoomed past me and _fire_ (past-tense verb) all over the catcher. After _2k15_ (large number) tries, I finally hit the _chicken_ (same fruit) all the way to _Orlando_ (faraway city). I started _ruging_ (verb ending in -ing) as fast as I could until I slid into home base. This new game isn't so _stinke_ (adjective) after all.

AWESOME
EXPLORATION

Wasfia Nazreen—Bangladeshi human rights activist and adventurer—paddles her canoe on the Columbia River Valley Wetlands, near Wilmer, British Columbia, Canada.

EARTH EXPLORER

Meet **Barrington Irving!**

This National Geographic emerging explorer dares kids to fly high.

Barrington Irving's soaring career hit high altitude when he was just 23 years old. That's when he set out to pilot a single-engine airplane on a trip spanning the globe. During that 97-day journey he navigated through thunderstorms, monsoons, snowstorms, and sandstorms—and eventually landed in the history books as the youngest person and the first African American to fly solo around the world.

Barrington's 2007 record has since been broken, but he has yet to stop inspiring kids around the globe to spread their wings and go after their own high-flying ambitions. As the "captain" of the Flying Classroom (flyingclassroom.com), Barrington visits students and shares his own experiences while offering real-life lessons in science, technology, engineering, and math (also known as STEM+).

"I use STEM+ in everything I do," says Irving, who has worked with middle school kids to create things like a car that goes from 0 to 60 miles an hour (96.6 km/h) in less than three seconds. "Kids can build anything!"

Barrington also believes kids can be anything, even if their dreams seem out of reach.

"I was always fascinated with planes as a kid but never thought I was smart enough to fly one," he says. "Then I randomly met an airline pilot named Capt. Gary Robinson. Interest turned into passion and I fell in love with aviation because someone believed in me."

Today, Irving hopes to pay it forward when it comes to supporting kids and getting them to believe in themselves.

"You have to have confidence," he says. "If you don't believe, no one else will. Confidence will always keep you going."

One trip around the world is about 30,000 miles (48,280 km) long.

IRVING READING NOTES FROM STUDENTS AS HE CROSSES THE EQUATOR

" Always be willing to explore beyond what you don't know and can ever dream of. Never let anything limit you from soaring. See the world! "

WORKING WITH THE INVASIVE CANE TOAD IN AUSTRALIA

During his 97-day trip around the world, Barrington made just 26 stops.

CALL TO ACTION!

Want to fly the friendly skies one day? You can build your knowledge base right in your own bedroom. "Start with YouTube videos [about flying and pilots]," suggests Barrington. Or, you can ask your parents to put you in touch with a pilot or someone who works in aviation. "I remember when I started I simply picked up the phone and would call offices to have a discussion with professionals," says Irving.

BARRINGTON AND CO-PILOT TOM

Meet Your Shark Bestie

Some sharks grow over 30,000 teeth in their lifetime.

YOU WON'T BELIEVE THESE PREDATOR PERSONALITIES.

While diving off the Bahama Islands, National Geographic photographer Brian Skerry noticed an oceanic whitetip shark swimming toward him. Soon the nine-foot (2.7-m)-long female was gently bumping her snout against Skerry's camera.

The shark's mouth was closed, so Skerry knew she wasn't trying to bite him. Instead, she just examined his photographic equipment like a curious kid. Skerry says this type of behavior shows that sharks have all sorts of personalities. And even individuals belonging to a species that's thought to be aggressive can have a major sweet side.

PERSONALITY POWER

Hiking in the Bahamas through a mangrove forest—a group of shrubs or trees that grow in coastal waters—Skerry arrived at a wild nursery for lemon shark pups in about a foot (0.3 m) of water. He put on his snorkel gear and scrambled onto his stomach to snap pics of the fish, watching as three shark pups swished closer to investigate. "Certain sharks are quicker to explore new things in their environment," Skerry says. Meaning some sharks are also super social, while others within the same species prefer their me time.

Different sharks within the same species thrive in different situations. Social lemon sharks may do better when food is plentiful because they'll share the grub with each other. But when food is scarce, the loner lemon sharks might thrive, since they don't divide their meals.

SUPERSIZE SHARK

On another diving trip, Skerry caught sight of a 14-foot (4.3-m)-long tiger shark in the Atlantic Ocean. Skerry admits to being nervous at first, but the shark just glided over him and actually allowed Skerry to touch her. The tiger shark, known as Emma, visited the dive site almost every day during Skerry's stay. "She was just a gentle giant," says Skerry.

Skerry hopes that by showing the different personalities of sharks, people will view them

SKERRY TOOK THIS PHOTO OF A LEMON SHARK PUP FROM THE WATERY FLOOR OF A MANGROVE FOREST.

More than 450 species of sharks exist, but at least 26 of them are endangered and at least 48 are vulnerable.

THIS PHOTO, TAKEN BY BRIAN SKERRY, SHOWS A DIVER INTERACTING WITH A TIGER SHARK OFF THE BAHAMA ISLANDS.

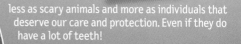

THE ULTIMATE BOOK OF SHARKS

Check out this book!

SKERRY READIES HIS CAMERA TO TAKE PHOTOS OF A SCHOOL OF CARIBBEAN REEF SHARKS.

less as scary animals and more as individuals that deserve our care and protection. Even if they do have a lot of teeth!

GUARDIANS OF THE SEA

Want to help keep coral reefs in good condition? Call in the sharks! Certain sharks eat animals that prey on herbivorous (or plant-eating) fish. Since herbivorous fish eat harmful algae that grow on the reefs, a break in that chain would be bad news for coral. Thank goodness for hungry sharks.

A REMORA FISH CATCHES A RIDE ON A TIGER SHARK OFF THE BAHAMA ISLANDS.

THE LOST SKULL

Bones found in a submerged Mexican cave give clues about the first Americans.

DIVER SUSAN BIRD CLEANS THE SKULL WITH A BRUSH.

A man once dived more than 900 feet (274 m) underwater without an oxygen supply.

I n 2007, a team of scuba divers swimming off Mexico's Yucatán Peninsula came across an eerie, but exciting find. Deep within an underwater cave, in a chamber the size of two basketball courts, was the oldest complete human skeleton ever found in the Americas. These ancient remains held clues to ultimately reveal new things about the first people to live in North America.

A JAW-DROPPING FIND

Experts suspected that the remains belonged to a teenage girl who lived in the last ice age some 12,000 years ago. They named her Naia, after a sea creature in Greek myths, and assessed that she likely died after falling into a large hole

caused by dropping sea levels and erosion. Over time, sea levels rose again and water flooded the cave, burying Naia for the next 12 millennia.

A LINK TO THE PAST

By examining the bones and other items found nearby like teeth, experts ran DNA tests to assess that Naia is a direct ancestor of present-day Native Americans. Naia's DNA also matches with people native to Siberia, a part of Russia. Scientists have long thought that ancient people from this region crossed to North America on land exposed between what is now Russia and Alaska during the last ice age. They were the first humans to inhabit the Americas, and Naia proves how far south they went.

Today, Naia's skull is in a lab. Researchers are still studying her skull to learn about early Americans, so she can continue to shed light on the past.

THE WATER IN WHICH NAIA WAS FOUND HELPED PRESERVE HER SKULL.

The Yucatán Peninsula has 2,500 Maya ruins.

NORTH AMERICA · ATLANTIC OCEAN
MEXICO
PACIFIC OCEAN
SOUTH AMERICA

UNITED STATES

MEXICO Gulf of Mexico

★ Mexico City Caribbean Sea

HOYO NEGRO

PACIFIC OCEAN

Out of This World

SCIENTISTS SPEND EIGHT MONTHS IN ISOLATION TO MIMIC LIFE ON MARS

What's life like on Mars? A crew of researchers have a pretty good idea about living on the red planet after spending eight straight months in a Mars-like habitat. In an initiative run by the University of Hawaii and sponsored by NASA, the six scientists lived inside a vinyl dome below the summit of Hawaii's Mauna Loa volcano, meant to mimic the rugged, rocky terrain on Mars.

JUST LIKE THE REAL DEAL

Eating mostly freeze-dried and canned food, the crew conducted surveys and experiments while practicing protocols for an actual mission to Mars, including fixing equipment, mapping, and even growing fresh vegetables. Any communication with the outside world was on a 20-minute delay—the time it takes for signals to travel between Earth and Mars. And anytime they left the dome to do fieldwork outside, they'd put on their spacesuits, just like they'd need to do while on Mars.

HEAD GAMES

The experiment also tested the crew's ability to be mostly cut off from the rest of the world. While the six of them bonded by playing games like Pictionary and watching movies together, it's hard to avoid conflict while living in isolation. Making matters a bit more, well, stressful? Sharing a space about the size of a two-bedroom home—including two composting toilets and one shower—a similar setup to what astronauts would have on Mars. Throughout the eight-month experiment, the team worked on practicing open and honest communication to resolve conflict so they could better focus on completing their tasks.

MISSION ACCOMPLISHED

While the mock mission may seem out of this world, NASA says the experiment and others like it will help it better plan and prepare for an actual trip to Mars, which may be just a decade or two away.

NATIONAL GEOGRAPHIC KiDS

ALMANAC CHALLENGE 2020

BE A 2020 VISIONARY!

A lot has happened in the world since the first *National Geographic Kids Almanac* was published 10 years ago. We've discovered evidence of water on Mars, mass-produced electric cars for consumers, and tracked the DNA sequence of the human genome. Smartphones took off and tons of apps were invented. Selfies, makerspaces, and 3D printers came into fashion.

In the past decade, National Geographic explorers have also accomplished great things to further our mission to understand and protect the planet. They've helped establish important new marine sanctuaries and national parks to preserve animal habitats and biodiversity all over the globe. These adventurers have explored the deepest realms of the ocean, and uncovered the oldest human fossils and new dinosaur species to shed light on the past—and the future.

PHOTO ARK
JOEL SARTORE

National Geographic photographer Joel Sartore is photographing every animal species in captivity for his Photo Ark project to show the wonder of all animals and inspire people to protect them.

A new species of human ancestor, called *Homo naledi,* was discovered by National Geographic Explorer Lee Berger and his team in a South African cave.

THIS YEAR'S CHALLENGE

To celebrate the Almanac's 10th anniversary, we invite you to be a 2020 Visionary. Think about the world 10 years from now, picture a positive change, invention, or discovery that you'd like to see happen, and share your vision with us. Focus on whatever you're interested in—animals, plants, people, places, science, medicine, technology, conservation. The sky's the limit! You don't have to be an expert on how to make your vision a reality. You just have to tell us what it is, how it would make the world better, and why it matters to you. Send us your visionary idea, and it could be featured in next year's Almanac!

Find inspiration and info on how to submit your entry at natgeokids.com/almanac.

LAST YEAR'S CHALLENGE

Check out the winner of last year's Lions Forever poster contest. We received more than 500 entries with amazing artwork and inspiring messages of conservation. Thanks to all the kids from around the world who entered and shared their interest in saving lions. See more entries at **natgeokids.com/almanac.**

WINNER

NORA B., AGE 12, SEVERNA PARK, MARYLAND, U.S.A.

RUNNERS-UP

(LEFT) MARIAM S., AGE 11, PRAIRIE VILLAGE, KANSAS, U.S.A.
(MIDDLE) SHABAD S., AGE 11, BOWIE, MARYLAND, U.S.A.
(RIGHT) LILAH P., AGE 10, ST. LOUIS, MISSOURI, U.S.A.

SEARCH-AND-RESCUE
D⊕G

SKI PATROLLER IVAN MCGURK TRAINS SHAKA THE GOLDEN RETRIEVER TO FIND LOST SKIERS AFTER AVALANCHES.

Have no fear, superdog is here!

SHAKA TAKES A BREAK FROM TRAINING AS MCGURK LOOKS ON.

North Lake Tahoe, California, U.S.A.

Shaka the golden retriever digs in the snow. He's not pawing through the snow for fun, though—he's practicing to save lives. That's because Shaka is part of Squaw Dogs, a team of search-and-rescue dogs at the Squaw Valley Ski Resort. The animals assist their human handlers with finding lost skiers after avalanches.

Shaka's handler, ski patroller Ivan McGurk, says that though humans can use their eyes to look for injured skiers aboveground, they need help to find people under the snow. "Shaka's trained to search for humans using his nose," McGurk says. "I need his sense of smell to track down what I can't see."

When Shaka's not working, he's with his best friend, Kaya the Belgian Malinois, another Squaw Dog. And when they play something called "flying squirrel," look out! "Shaka runs at Kaya and leaps on her!" says Ben Stone, Kaya's handler. He saves lives *and* he can fly? Someone get this dog a cape.

HOW TO
SURVIVE ...

A LION ATTACK

1 CATFIGHT
Lions usually avoid confrontations with people. But if one lunges toward you, **swing a tree branch, throw rocks, even gouge its eyes.** Fighting back may make it slink away like the Cowardly Lion.

2 DON'T TAKE IT "LION DOWN"
Never crouch, kneel, or play dead. The lion might think you're ready to become a Kid McNugget.

3 ACT LIKE A PRO WRESTLER
Lions go after weaker prey, so show it that you rule. **Scream, snarl, and bare your teeth** (even if you have braces). Come on stronger than The Rock in a smackdown.

4 STRENGTH IN NUMBERS
Lions prefer to attack solitary prey, so make sure you safari with plenty of friends. Don't let the lion divide and conquer— **keep your pals close by at all times.**

5 SEE YA LATER
See an escape route? Don't wait for a permission slip, Einstein! **Slowly back away—but never turn tail and run.** You just might avoid a major *cat*-astrophe.

QUICKSAND

1 NO MORE *SOUP-*ERSTITIONS
Quicksand isn't some bottomless pit waiting to suck you in. It's a soupy mixture of sand and water found near riverbanks, shorelines, and marshes. It's rarely more than a few feet deep, though it can be deeper.

2 GO WITH THE FLOAT
Not that you'd want to, but quicksand is actually **easier to float on than water.** So lean back, place your arms straight out from your sides, and let the sopping sand support your weight.

3 YOU FLAIL, YOU FAIL
Don't kick or struggle. That creates a vacuum, which only pulls you down. Ignore the gritty goop squishing into your underpants and remain calm.

4 LEG LIFTS
Conquer the quicksand with **a slow stand.** As you're lying back with your arms out, carefully inch one leg, then the other, to the surface.

5 ROLL OVER!
When both legs are afloat, pretend you're performing a dog trick. Keeping your face out of the muck, **gently roll over the quicksand** until you're on solid ground.

awes8me
EXTREME SPORTS

CLIFF JUMPERS!

1 TAKE THE PLUNGE

Cannonball! A brave diver leaps off the La Quebrada Cliffs in Acapulco, Mexico. The height of the jump? Some 150 feet (45.7 m)—four times taller than most platform diving boards.

2 WINGING IT

At the World BASE Race, competitors soar from cliffs wearing wingsuits. Free-falling faster than a speeding train for about two minutes, the jumpers eventually pull a parachute to glide gently to the ground.

3 CURVE APPEAL

Cars and motorcycles drive sideways along a wall in this dizzying display in India. Thanks to centripetal force, vehicles stay stuck to the wall as they loop around the curved course.

4 GO WITH THE FLOW

This sport is on fire. In ash boarding, you strap a wooden board onto your feet before shooting down the slope of an active volcano, reaching speeds up to 50 miles an hour (80.5 km/h).

5 WHEELS UP

Rock 'n' roll! A free rider sails over a steep rock wall in Moab, Utah, U.S.A. In free riding, cyclists use obstacles in nature—like rock formations and twisty trails—to do daring tricks and stunts.

6 BALANCING ACT

No fear here: A daredevil tiptoes along a wire as she crosses between two cliffs in the Italian Alps. A stumble at this height would be like falling from the top of the Empire State Building.

7 THROWN FOR A LOOP

Stunt cyclist Danny MacAskill seems to defy gravity by riding around a 16-foot (4.9-m)-tall loop. Here, he's shown in a time-lapsed photo making a full circle before riding away on his bike.

8 BIG AIR

A snowboarder is flying high during the slopestyle event at the 2014 Winter Olympics in Sochi, Russia. Slopestyle competitors race down a mountain dotted with obstacles like ramps, which allow them to catch major air.

DUH! Don't try these tricks on your own.

PHOTO TIPS:
Getting Started

TAKING A PHOTO IS AS EASY AS PUSHING A BUTTON, but taking a good photo requires patience and a general understanding of how photography works. Whether you're using a low-end smartphone or a high-end digital camera, check out National Geographic photographer Annie Griffith's top tips and tricks for taking better pictures. With these expert pointers, you'll discover how to get the shot you want.

TIP 1

Get Closer When You Photograph People

Remember, it's the face of a person that makes us love people pictures, not their shoes! So move in close and show that beautiful face!

TIP 2

Take Time to Think About Your Composition

Composition is the way you place objects or people inside the frame. This is where you can be most creative. Remember, what is left OUT of the frame is as important as what is left in, so look carefully to see if anything in the shot will distract from your subject. If so, find a way to recompose, or rearrange, the photo so the distraction is left out.

composition:
the arrangement of the subject and its surroundings in a frame

TIP 3

Get Moving!

If you have taken lots of shots from one spot, try looking at the subject from another angle: above, behind, close up, far away. Professional photographers are moving all the time, always trying for a better shot.

TIP 4

Don't Photograph People in the Sun

Bright sun is usually the worst light for photographing people. The sun causes deep shadows and harsh light. Besides, everyone in the picture is usually squinting! It's much better to move your subjects to a shady spot where the light is softer.

TIP 5

Quality Not Quantity

It's far better to take fewer, more thoughtfully composed pictures, than it is to shoot like a maniac. It's not about how many pictures you take. It's about how cool those pictures are!

GUIDE TO
PHOTO
GRAPHY

Check out the book!

197

QUIZ WHIZ

Discover just how much you know about exploration with this quiz!

Write your answers on a piece of paper. Then check them below.

1 More than _____ species of sharks exist.
a. 45
b. 260
c. 450
d. 700

2 **True or false?** It's easier to float on quicksand than water.

3 Which location has a rocky terrain that's similar to Mars?
a. Chile
b. Hawaii
c. Mongolia
d. Tunisia

4 Bright _____ is usually the worst light for photographing people.

5 In _____ boarding, you strap a wooden board to your feet and shoot down an active volcano.
a. hot
b. ash
c. lava
d. snow

Not **STUMPED** yet? Check out the *NATIONAL GEOGRAPHIC KIDS QUIZ WHIZ* collection for more crazy **EXPLORATION** questions!

ANSWERS: 1. c; 2. True 3. b; 4. sun; 5. b

HOMEWORK HELP

How to Write a Perfect Essay

Need to write an essay? Does the assignment feel as big as climbing Mount Everest? Fear not. You're up to the challenge! The following step-by-step tips will help you with this monumental task.

1 **BRAINSTORM.** Sometimes the subject matter of your essay is assigned to you, sometimes it's not. Either way, you have to decide what you want to say. Start by brainstorming some ideas, writing down any thoughts you have about the subject. Then read over everything you've come up with and consider which idea you think is the strongest. Ask yourself what you want to write about the most. Keep in mind the goal of your essay. Can you achieve the goal of the assignment with this topic? If so, you're good to go.

2 **WRITE A TOPIC SENTENCE.** This is the main idea of your essay, a statement of your thoughts on the subject. Again, consider the goal of your essay. Think of the topic sentence as an introduction that tells your reader what the rest of your essay will be about.

3 **OUTLINE YOUR IDEAS.** Once you have a good topic sentence, you then need to support that main idea with more detailed information, facts, thoughts, and examples. These supporting points answer one question about your topic sentence—"Why?" This is where research and perhaps more brainstorming come in. Then organize these points in the way you think makes the most sense, probably in order of importance. Now you have an outline for your essay.

4 **ON YOUR MARK, GET SET, WRITE!** Follow your outline, using each of your supporting points as the topic sentence of its own paragraph. Use descriptive words to get your ideas across to the reader. Go into detail, using specific information to tell your story or make your point. Stay on track, making sure that everything you include is somehow related to the main idea of your essay. Use transitions to make your writing flow.

5 **WRAP IT UP.** Finish your essay with a conclusion that summarizes your entire essay and restates your main idea.

6 **PROOFREAD AND REVISE.** Check for errors in spelling, capitalization, punctuation, and grammar. Look for ways to make your writing clear, understandable, and interesting. Use descriptive verbs, adjectives, or adverbs when possible. It also helps to have someone else read your work to point out things you might have missed. Then make the necessary corrections and changes in a second draft. Repeat this revision process once more to make your final draft as good as you can.

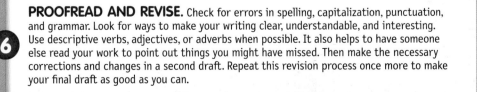

Lightning flashes above Monument Valley Navajo Tribal Park on the border of Arizona and Utah, U.S.A.

EARTH EXPLORER
Meet **Enric Sala!**

This National Geographic explorer-in-residence is fighting to save the world's oceans, one fish at a time.

Picture this: You're diving off the coast of Costa Rica when you look up to see 200 hammerhead sharks swimming above you. Later, you slowly cruise through a school of some 100 whitetip reef sharks, before setting your gaze on a pod of giant whale sharks—all in the same pocket of the Pacific Ocean.

This is what Enric Sala, a National Geographic explorer-in-residence, experienced on a recent dive trip off Cocos Island, a national park about 330 miles (530 km) from Costa Rica's mainland. As a marine ecologist, Enric travels the world studying the world's oceans and working to save marine life.

As amazing as some of those trips are, Enric has seen things that turned his career into his passion. He has seen sharks pierced with rusty steel hooks, whales washed up on shores with their bellies full of plastic, and coral reefs dying off at an alarming rate.

"Humans are destroying ocean life because of too much fishing, pollution, and climate change," says Enric. "But if we protect the ocean, marine life can come back."

Through his Pristine Seas project, Enric is hoping to save the oceans. He and his team are setting up Marine Protected Areas (MPAs) throughout the world. Like national parks on land, these are safe spaces in the ocean where human activities, like fishing, are strictly regulated.

So far, the Pristine Seas project has helped to establish 19 marine reserves across the globe, in spots like Russia and Chile. Still, less than 5 percent of the world's oceans are officially protected. But Enric is hopeful that number will continue to increase as people become more and more aware of the desperate need to save the oceans—and everything in them.

"The ocean is vital to our survival as it gives us food, more than half of the oxygen we breathe, and many more wonderful things," says Enric.

RAINBOW WRASSES IN THE MEDITERRANEAN SEA

About 70 percent of Earth's surface is covered with water.

" In only three years, we can see already more fish than before. In ten years, the abundance of fish inside a protected area is, on average, six times greater than outside. Everything comes back. "

GREEN SEA TURTLE, COCOS ISLAND, COSTA RICA

The Mariana Trench, the deepest part of the ocean, is deeper than Mount Everest is tall.

CALL TO ACTION!

"Go in the ocean, swim, and snorkel. Or just go to any place where you can enjoy the natural world," says Enric. "Take a walk through a forest, explore a marsh, or run through a prairie. Spend time in nature and you'll fall in love with it."

TABUAERAN LAGOON, KIRIBATI

Weather and Climate

Weather is the condition of the atmosphere—temperature, wind, humidity, and precipitation—at a given place at a given time. Climate, however, is the average weather for a particular place over a long period of time. Different places on Earth have different climates, but climate is not a random occurrence. It is a pattern that is controlled by factors such as latitude, elevation, prevailing winds, the temperature of ocean currents, and location on land relative to water. Climate is generally constant, but evidence indicates that human activity is causing a change in its patterns.

WOW-WORTHY WEATHER

CANADIAN COLD SNAP: In December 2017, Toronto, Canada, cracked a 57-year-old weather record with temperatures dropping to minus 7.6°F (-22°C).

SEEING ORANGE: Dark orange snow sometimes falls on parts of Europe, the result of storms blowing dust from the Sahara into the atmosphere, where it mixes with the white stuff.

RECORD RAIN: A record-setting rainstorm soaked the Hawaiian island of Kauai in April 2018, with nearly 50 inches (127 cm) of rain falling in just one 24-hour period.

GLOBAL CLIMATE ZONES

Climatologists, people who study climate, have created different systems for classifying climates. One that is often used is called the Köppen system, which classifies climate zones according to precipitation, temperature, and vegetation. It has five major categories—Tropical, Dry, Temperate, Cold, and Polar—with a sixth category for locations where high elevations override other factors.

ARCTIC OCEAN

ARCTIC CIRCLE

TROPIC OF CANCER

ATLANTIC OCEAN

PACIFIC OCEAN

EQUATOR

PACIFIC OCEAN

TROPIC OF CAPRICORN

INDIAN OCEAN

ANTARCTIC CIRCLE

Climate

Tropical | Dry | Humid temperate | Humid cold | Polar

EXTREME CLIMATES

Talk about a temperature swing! The difference between the coldest place on Earth—east Antarctica—and the hottest—Death Valley, in Nevada and California, U.S.A.—is a whopping 270°F (150°C). Though they are both deserts, these two opposites are neck and neck in the race for world's most extreme climate.

HOT
DEATH VALLEY

CRAZY TEMPS	Hottest temperature ever recorded: **134°F** (57°C)
RAINFALL	Death Valley is the driest place in North America. The average yearly rainfall is about **2 inches (5 cm)**.
ELEVATION	At **282 feet (86 m) below sea level**, Death Valley is the lowest point in North America.
STEADY HEAT	In 2001, Death Valley experienced **160 consecutive days** of temperatures **100°F (38°C)** or hotter.

COLD
EAST ANTARCTIC PLATEAU

CRAZY TEMPS	Coldest temperature ever recorded: **-135.8°F** (-93°C)
RAINFALL	East Antarctica gets less than **2 inches (5 cm)** of precipitation in a year.
ELEVATION	The record low temperature was recorded just below the plateau's **13,000-foot (3,962-m)** ridge.
DARKNESS	During parts of winter, there is **24 hours** of darkness.

WATER CYCLE

Precipitation falls

Water storage in ice and snow

Water vapor condenses in clouds

Water filters into the ground

Meltwater and surface runoff

Freshwater storage

Evaporation

Groundwater discharge

Water storage in ocean

The amount of water on Earth is more or less constant—

only the form changes. As the sun warms Earth's surface, liquid water is changed into water vapor in a process called **evaporation**. Water on the surface of plants' leaves turns into water vapor in a process called **transpiration**. As water vapor rises into the air, it cools and changes form again. This time, it becomes clouds in a process called **condensation**. Water droplets fall from the clouds as **precipitation**, which then travels as groundwater or runoff back to the lakes, rivers, and oceans, where the cycle (shown above) starts all over again.

To a meteorologist— a person who studies the weather— a "light rain" is less than 1/48 inch (0.5 mm). A "heavy rain" is more than 1/6 inch (4 mm).

You drink the same water as the dinosaurs! Earth has been recycling water for more than four billion years.

206

Types of Clouds

If you want a clue about the weather, look up at the clouds. They'll tell a lot about the condition of the air and what weather might be on the way. Clouds are made of both air and water. On fair days, warm air currents rise up and push against the water in clouds, keeping it from falling. But as the raindrops in a cloud get bigger, it's time to set them free. The bigger raindrops become too heavy for the air currents to hold up, and they fall to the ground.

How Much Does a Cloud Weigh?

A light, fluffy cumulus cloud typically weighs about 216,000 pounds (98,000 kg). That's about the weight of 18 elephants. A rain-soaked cumulonimbus cloud typically weighs 105.8 million pounds (48 million kg), or about the same as 9,000 elephants.

1 STRATUS These clouds make the sky look like a bowl of thick gray porridge. They hang low in the sky, blanketing the day in dreary darkness. Stratus clouds form when cold, moist air close to the ground moves over a region.

2 CIRRUS These wispy tufts of clouds are thin and hang high up in the atmosphere where the air is extremely cold. Cirrus clouds are made of tiny ice crystals.

3 CUMULONIMBUS These are the monster clouds. Rising air currents force fluffy cumulus clouds to swell and shoot upward, as much as 70,000 feet (21,000 m). When these clouds bump against the top of the troposphere, or the tropopause, they flatten out on top like tabletops.

4 CUMULUS These white, fluffy clouds make people sing, "Oh, what a beautiful morning!" They form low in the atmosphere and look like marshmallows. They often mix with large patches of blue sky. Formed when hot air rises, cumulus clouds usually disappear when the air cools at night.

207

HURRICANE
HAPPENINGS

A storm is coming! But is it a tropical cyclone, a hurricane, or a typhoon? These weather events go by different names depending on where they form and how fast their winds get. Strong tropical cyclones are called hurricanes in the Atlantic and parts of the Pacific Ocean; in the western Pacific they are called typhoons. But any way you look at it, these storms pack a punch.

1,380 MILES (2,221 km)

diameter of the most massive tropical cyclone ever recorded, 1979's Typhoon Tip

82°F (27.8°C)

water surface temperature necessary for a tropical cyclone to form

16.6

average number of tropical storms each year in the Northeast and Central Pacific Basins

10

number of Hurricane Sandy–related pictures uploaded every second to Instagram on October 29, 2012

31

number of days Hurricane John lasted in 1994

12.1

average number of tropical storms
in the Atlantic Basin each year

254
MPH

(408 km/h)

strongest gust of storm wind
ever recorded

12-25
MILES

(20–40 km)

diameter of a hurricane eye

HURRICANE NAMES FOR 2020

Hurricane names come from six official international
lists. The names alternate between male and female.
When a storm becomes a hurricane, a name from the
list is used, in alphabetical order. Each list is reused
every six years. A name "retires" if that hurricane
caused a lot of damage or many deaths. Check out
the names for 2020.

Arthur	Hanna	Omar
Bertha	Isaias	Paulette
Cristobal	Josephine	Rene
Dolly	Kyle	Sally
Edouard	Laura	Teddy
Fay	Marco	Vicky
Gonzalo	Nana	Wilfred

SCALE OF HURRICANE INTENSITY

CATEGORY	ONE	TWO	THREE	FOUR	FIVE
DAMAGE	Minimal	Moderate	Extensive	Extreme	Catastrophic
WINDS	74–95 mph (119–153 km/h)	96–110 mph (154–177 km/h)	111–129 mph (178–208 km/h)	130–156 mph (209–251 km/h)	157 mph or higher (252+ km/h)
(DAMAGE refers to wind and water damage combined.)					

HURRICANE!

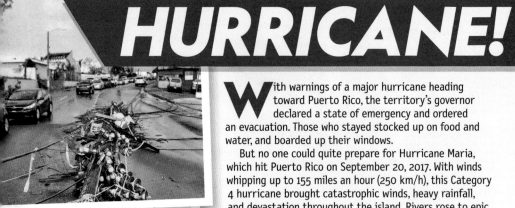

With warnings of a major hurricane heading toward Puerto Rico, the territory's governor declared a state of emergency and ordered an evacuation. Those who stayed stocked up on food and water, and boarded up their windows.

But no one could quite prepare for Hurricane Maria, which hit Puerto Rico on September 20, 2017. With winds whipping up to 155 miles an hour (250 km/h), this Category 4 hurricane brought catastrophic winds, heavy rainfall, and devastation throughout the island. Rivers rose to epic heights, buildings were destroyed, and power was wiped out across nearly the entire island. An estimated 2,975 people died as a result of the storm, with hundreds of others injured. All told, Maria was Puerto Rico's worst ever natural disaster.

For months, thousands of people remained without power, cell service, or internet as electrical grids and utility towers were slowly repaired or replaced. The storm racked up some $90 billion in damage, making it one of the most costly hurricanes ever.

After receiving support from around the world, Puerto Rico has begun to recover. Six months after the storm took out a road through Puerto Rico's popular El Yunque rain forest, parts of the park reopened. It's a promising sign that life is returning to usual on this island.

EARTHQUAKE!

In the wee hours of Monday, February 26, 2018, life was quiet in Papua New Guinea. But at 3:44 a.m., a powerful 7.5 earthquake split the ground open and devastated the nation in an instant.

Roads became impassable. Homes crumbled to the ground. Landslides caused contamination of safe drinking water. The quake destroyed crops and vegetable gardens, cutting off the primary food sources for a significant percentage of Papua New Guinea's 8.3 million citizens. Significant aftershocks, which lasted into March, caused additional damage.

With thousands of people impacted—and a death toll of more than 100—humanitarian groups such as World Food Programme stepped in to supply food, medical care, and other much needed aid. Countries such as Australia and New Zealand committed funding as well as the use of their military planes.

While the recovery after a natural disaster never happens right away, these types of efforts are helping Papua New Guinea piece itself back together.

THE ENHANCED FUJITA SCALE

The Enhanced Fujita (EF) Scale, named after tornado expert T. Theodore Fujita, classifies tornadoes based on wind speed and the intensity of damage that they cause.

What is a tornado?

EF0
65–85 mph winds
(105–137 km/h)
Slight damage

EF1
86–110 mph winds
(138–177 km/h)
Moderate damage

EF2
111–135 mph winds
(178–217 km/h)
Substantial damage

EF3
136–165 mph winds
(218–266 km/h)
Severe damage

EF4
166–200 mph winds
(267–322 km/h)
Massive damage

EF5
More than 200 mph winds
(322+ km/h)
Catastrophic damage

TORNADOES, ALSO KNOWN AS TWISTERS, are funnels of rapidly rotating air that are created during a thunderstorm. With wind speeds of up to 300 miles an hour (483 km/h), tornadoes have the power to pick up and destroy everything in their path.

THIS ROTATING FUNNEL OF AIR, formed in a cumulus or cumulonimbus cloud, becomes a tornado if it touches the ground.

TORNADOES HAVE OCCURRED IN ALL 50 U.S. STATES AND ON EVERY CONTINENT EXCEPT ANTARCTICA.

Biomes

A BIOME, OFTEN CALLED A MAJOR LIFE ZONE, is one of the natural world's major communities where plants and animals adapt to their specific surroundings. Biomes are classified depending on the predominant vegetation, climate, and geography of a region. They can be divided into six major types: forest, freshwater, marine, desert, grassland, and tundra. Each biome consists of many ecosystems.

Biomes are extremely important. Balanced ecological relationships among biomes help to maintain the environment and life on Earth as we know it. For example, an increase in one species of plant, such as an invasive one, can cause a ripple effect throughout a whole biome.

FOREST

Forests occupy about one-third of Earth's land area. There are three major types of forests: tropical, temperate, and boreal (taiga). Forests are home to a diversity of plants, some of which may hold medicinal qualities for humans, as well as thousands of animal species, some still undiscovered. Forests can also absorb carbon dioxide, a greenhouse gas, and give off oxygen.

The rabbit-size royal antelope lives in West Africa's dense forests.

FRESHWATER

Most water on Earth is salty, but freshwater ecosystems—including lakes, ponds, wetlands, rivers, and streams—usually contain water with less than one percent salt concentration. The countless animal and plant species that live in freshwater biomes vary from continent to continent, but they include algae, frogs, turtles, fish, and the larvae of many insects.

The place where fresh and salt water meet is called an estuary.

MARINE

The marine biome covers almost three-fourths of Earth's surface, making it the largest habitat on our planet. Oceans make up the majority of the saltwater marine biome. Coral reefs are considered to be the most biodiverse of any of the biome habitats. The marine biome is home to more than one million plant and animal species.

Estimated to be up to 100,000 years old, sea grass growing in the Mediterranean Sea may be the oldest living thing on Earth.

DESERT

Covering about one-fifth of Earth's surface, deserts are places where precipitation is less than 10 inches (25 cm) per year. Although most deserts are hot, there are other kinds as well. The four major kinds of deserts are hot, semiarid, coastal, and cold. Far from being barren wastelands, deserts are biologically rich habitats.

Some sand dunes in the Sahara are tall enough to bury a 50-story building.

GRASSLAND

Biomes called grasslands are characterized by having grasses instead of large shrubs or trees. Grasslands generally have precipitation for only about half to three-fourths of the year. If it were more, they would become forests. Grasslands can be divided into two types: tropical (savannas) and temperate. Some of the world's largest land animals, such as elephants, live there.

Grasslands in North America are called prairies; in South America, they're called pampas.

TUNDRA

The coldest of all biomes, a tundra is characterized by an extremely cold climate, simple vegetation, little precipitation, poor nutrients, and a short growing season. There are two types of tundra: arctic and alpine. A tundra is home to few kinds of vegetation. Surprisingly, though, there are quite a few animal species that can survive the tundra's extremes, such as wolves, caribou, and even mosquitoes.

Formed 10,000 years ago, the arctic tundra is the world's youngest biome.

THE OC

PACIFIC OCEAN

STATS

Surface area
65,436,200 sq mi (169,479,000 sq km)

Portion of Earth's water area
47 percent

Greatest depth
Challenger Deep
(in the Mariana Trench)
-36,070 ft (-10,994 m)

Surface temperatures
Summer high: 90°F (32°C)
Winter low: 28°F (-2°C)

Tides
Highest: 30 ft (9 m) near Korean Peninsula
Lowest: 1 ft (0.3 m) near Midway Islands

Cool creatures: giant Pacific octopus, bottlenose whale, clownfish, great white shark

ATLANTIC OCEAN

STATS

Surface area
35,338,500 sq mi (91,526,300 sq km)

Portion of Earth's water area
25 percent

Greatest depth
Puerto Rico Trench
-28,232 ft (-8,605 m)

Surface temperatures
Summer high: 90°F (32°C)
Winter low: 28°F (-2°C)

Tides
Highest: 52 ft (16 m)
Bay of Fundy, Canada
Lowest: 1.5 ft (0.5 m)
Gulf of Mexico and Mediterranean Sea

Cool creatures: blue whale, Atlantic spotted dolphin, sea turtle

CLOWN ANEMONEFISH

BOTTLENOSE DOLPHIN

EANS

INDIAN OCEAN

STATS

Surface area
28,839,800 sq mi (74,694,800 sq km)

Portion of Earth's water area
21 percent

Greatest depth
Java Trench
-23,376 ft (-7,125 m)

Surface temperatures
Summer high: 93°F (34°C)
Winter low: 28°F (-2°C)

Tides
Highest: 36 ft (11 m)
Lowest: 2 ft (0.6 m)
Both along Australia's west coast

Cool creatures: humpback whale, Portuguese
man-of-war, dugong (sea cow)

ARCTIC OCEAN

STATS

Surface area
5,390,000 sq mi (13,960,100 sq km)

Portion of Earth's water area
4 percent

Greatest depth
Molloy Deep
-18,599 ft (-5,669 m)

Surface temperatures
Summer high: 41°F (5°C)
Winter low: 28°F (-2°C)

Tides
Less than 1 ft (0.3 m) variation
throughout the ocean

Cool creatures: beluga whale, orca, harp
seal, narwhal

LEATHERBACK TURTLE

NARWHAL

To see the major oceans and bays in relation to landmasses, look at the map on pages 258 and 259.

Coral Reefs

Just below the surface of the Caribbean Sea's crystal clear water, miles of vivid corals grow in fantastic shapes that shelter tropical fish of every color. Coral reefs account for a quarter of all life in the ocean and are often called the rain forests of the sea. Like big apartment complexes for sea creatures, coral reefs provide a tough limestone skeleton for fish, clams, and other organisms to live in—and plenty of food for them to eat, too.

And how does the coral get its color? It's all about the algae that cling to its limestone polyps. Algae and coral live together in a mutually helpful relationship. The coral provides a home to the algae and helps the algae convert sunlight into food that the corals consume. But as beautiful as coral reefs are, they are also highly sensitive. A jump of even 2°F (1.1°C) in water temperature makes the reef rid itself of the algae, leaving the coral with a sickly, bleached look. Pollution is another threat; it can poison the sensitive corals. Humans pose a threat, too: One clumsy kick from a swimmer can destroy decades of coral growth.

SEA STAR
ON A SPONGE

QUEEN
ANGELFISH

BY THE NUMBERS

25 percent of all marine creatures are supported by coral reefs.

500 million is how many years ago the world's first coral reefs formed.

4 is the number of countries that border the Mesoamerican Barrier Reef: Mexico, Honduras, Belize, and Guatemala.

THE

GREAT
BARRIER
REEF
IN
AUSTRALIA
IS THE
BIGGEST
LIVING
STRUCTURE
ON EARTH.

MANTA RAY

Try This!

CREATE A
MOTION OCEAN

Shake the jar and watch waves appear!

YOU WILL NEED
- clear jar with lid
- water
- blue food coloring
- glitter
- baby oil
- plastic floating toy

WHAT TO DO
1. Fill the jar halfway with water.
2. Add drops of food coloring until you like the color you see. Shake in a little glitter.
3. Pour in baby oil until the jar is three-quarters full.
4. Place a floating toy on top of the oil, then screw on the lid tightly.
5. Shake the jar gently to set your ocean in motion.

QUIZ WHIZ

Quiz yourself to find out if you're a natural when it comes to nature knowledge!

Write your answers on a piece of paper. Then check them below.

1 **True or false?** Wispy cirrus clouds usually appear where the air is warm.

2 The Fujita scale measures the speed and intensity of which type of storm?
a. blizzard
b. tornado
c. hurricane
d. typhoon

3 The world's first coral reefs formed some _____ years ago.
a. 5,000
b. 500,000
c. 500 million
d. 5 billion

4 **True or false?** Hurricane John lasted for 31 days in 1994.

5 What is the place called where freshwater and salt water meet?
a. estuary
b. tributary
c. tide pool
d. basin

Not **STUMPED** yet? Check out the *NATIONAL GEOGRAPHIC KIDS QUIZ WHIZ* collection for more crazy **NATURE** questions!

ANSWERS: 1. False, they appear where the air is cold; 2. b; 3. c; 4. True; 5. a

Oral Reports Made Easy

TIP:
Make sure you practice your presentation a few times. Stand in front of a mirror or have a parent record you so you can see if you need to work on anything, such as eye contact.

Does the thought of public speaking start your stomach churning like a tornado? Would you rather get caught in an avalanche than give a speech?

Giving an oral report does not have to be a natural disaster. The basic format is very similar to that of a written essay. There are two main elements that make up a good oral report—the writing and the presentation. As you write your oral report, remember that your audience will be hearing the information as opposed to reading it. Follow the guidelines below, and there will be clear skies ahead.

Writing Your Material

Follow the steps in the "How to Write a Perfect Essay" section on p. 199, but prepare your report to be spoken rather than written.

Try to keep your sentences short and simple. Long, complex sentences are harder to follow. Limit yourself to just a few key points. You don't want to overwhelm your audience with too much information. To be most effective, hit your key points in the introduction, elaborate on them in the body, and then repeat them once again in your conclusion.

AN ORAL REPORT HAS THREE BASIC PARTS:

- **Introduction**—This is your chance to engage your audience and really capture their interest in the subject you are presenting. Use a funny personal experience or a dramatic story, or start with an intriguing question.

- **Body**—This is the longest part of your report. Here you elaborate on the facts and ideas you want to convey. Give information that supports your main idea, and expand on it with specific examples or details. In other words, structure your oral report in the same way you would a written essay, so that your thoughts are presented in a clear and organized manner.

- **Conclusion**—This is the time to summarize the information and emphasize your most important points to the audience one last time.

Preparing Your Delivery

1 Practice makes perfect. Practice! Practice! Practice! Confidence, enthusiasm, and energy are key to delivering an effective oral report, and they can best be achieved through rehearsal. Ask family and friends to be your practice audience and give you feedback when you're done. Were they able to follow your ideas? Did you seem knowledgeable and confident? Did you speak too slowly or too fast, too softly or too loudly? The more times you practice giving your report, the more you'll master the material. Then you won't have to rely so heavily on your notes or papers, and you will be able to give your report in a relaxed and confident manner.

2 Present with everything you've got. Be as creative as you can. Incorporate videos, sound clips, slide presentations, charts, diagrams, and photos. Visual aids help stimulate your audience's senses and keep them intrigued and engaged. They can also help to reinforce your key points. And remember that when you're giving an oral report, you're a performer. Take charge of the spotlight and be as animated and entertaining as you can. Have fun with it.

3 Keep your nerves under control. Everyone gets a little nervous when speaking in front of a group. That's normal. But the more preparation you've done— meaning plenty of researching, organizing, and rehearsing—the more confident you'll be. Preparation is the key. And if you make a mistake or stumble over your words, just regroup and keep going. Nobody's perfect, and nobody expects you to be.

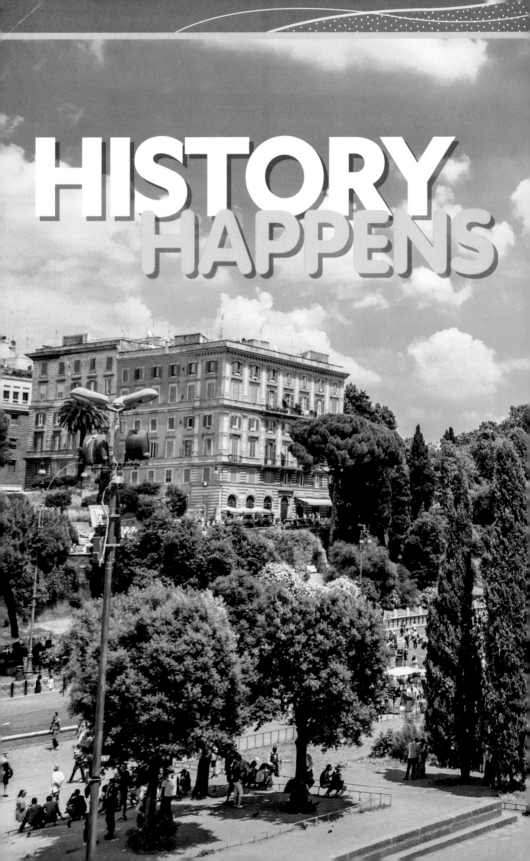

An amphitheater opened by Emperor Titus in A.D. 80, the Colosseum is among Rome, Italy's most visited monuments today.

EARTH EXPLORER
Meet Guillermo de Anda!

The National Geographic emerging explorer dives deep to discover what lies beneath.

Guillermo de Anda's life changed the first time he laid eyes on a submerged human skull. Buried deep inside an underwater cave, this ancient remain intrigued Guillermo—and directed the course of his career.

"That discovery made me want to dedicate my work to underwater archaeology and the study of ancient humans and civilizations," says Guillermo, whose team recently discovered the world's largest underwater cave system in Mexico.

Guillermo's work focuses on the ancient Maya civilization, and his expeditions are centered around cavelike pools called cenotes, which were once used in ancient rituals. In the murky depths of these cenotes, he has found the remains of extinct elephants, saber-toothed cats, and giant sloths—nearly perfectly preserved for as many as 15,000 years.

In particular, Guillermo highlights the Holtun Cenote in Chichén Itzá, Mexico, which contained the well-preserved remains of human and animal bones as well as jade and ceramics. Because cenotes date back thousands and thousands of years, exploring them may reveal more about the mysterious Maya.

"I am working to get a better understanding of the development of life and civilization over the last 20,000 years," says Guillermo. "Underwater archaeology is amazing, and the potential for research is endless."

GUILLERMO AT A MAYA ARCHAEOLOGICAL SITE IN MEXICO

The world's largest underwater cave is 216 miles (347 km) long.

GUILLERMO IN A CENOTE CALLED "EL PIT"

" One of my biggest career highlights to date is the discovery of the first bears found in Mexico's Yucatán Peninsula. We didn't know they ever existed in this area, and they turned out to be over 12,000 years old. "

DIVING IN A CENOTE IN YUCATÁN, MEXICO

Guillermo's team discovered more than 120 artifacts in one cenote, including ceramics and burnt human bones—all dating back some 12,000 years.

CALL TO ACTION!

Before you dive into underwater archaeology, Guillermo suggests you first learn all you can about archaeology in general. "Read books about the Ice Age, about the Maya civilization, and other parts of our past so that you know about a lot of different subjects," he says. As for a specific underwater career, you obviously have to be comfy taking the plunge. Guillermo says learning to scuba dive at an early age is key to avoiding fear when you're swimming through dark spaces. And to keep tabs on Guillermo and his team's progress in Mexico, check out granacuiferomaya.com.

Buried Secrets

Who built this ancient Egyptian monument?

A huge stone lion looms over the passing boats on Egypt's Nile River. It serves as a giant guardian to some of the country's famous pyramids, human-made tombs that seem to stretch all the way to the sun. The ancient sand-colored statue known as the Sphinx is as tall as the White House, with paws longer than a city bus.

How many hidden chambers are inside? Scientists are still digging up clues to answer that question, but they might have an answer for one of the monument's biggest mysteries: Who built it?

SET IN STONE

In ancient Egypt, people worshipped sphinxes as mythical creatures with the power to ward off evil. Some think the Sphinx was built as a protector of the pyramids, which were once used as burial places for Egyptian kings. Nobody's sure when the Sphinx was built, but experts believe it was already ancient when Egyptian queen Cleopatra saw it around 47 B.C. Since then, many other historical figures have visited the monument. But which historical figure *built* the monument?

FACE OFF

Historians' two top suspects are Pharaoh Khufu, who ruled Egypt from 2589 B.C. to 2566 B.C., and his son, Pharaoh Khafre, who reigned from 2558 B.C. to 2532 B.C. Most experts agree that one of these rulers oversaw the construction of the statue and had his own face carved atop the giant lion. But which one was it—Khufu or Khafre?

Some think the Sphinx is the work of Khufu. They say the statue's face matches a sculpture of the king discovered in 1903.

But most experts, including Egyptologist Mark Lehner, think Khufu's son, Khafre, built the Sphinx. As father and son, the pair shared a resemblance.

HISTORIANS THINK THE SPHINX MIGHT'VE LOOKED LIKE THIS BEFORE WIND AND WATER WORE AWAY ITS COLORS.

THE SPHINX SITS NEAR SIX PYRAMIDS, INCLUDING THE GREAT PYRAMID OF GIZA.

THE STATUE WASN'T FULLY UNCOVERED UNTIL 1936, ABOUT 70 YEARS AFTER THIS PIC WAS TAKEN.

Egypt's Nile River is the world's longest river, flowing over 4,400 miles (7,081 km) through eastern Africa.

Early Egyptians named their land Kemet, or "black land," for its rich river mud.

In Egypt, camels are called "ships of the desert." Like ships, they carry goods and people.

ATLANTIC OCEAN
EUROPE
ASIA
EGYPT
AFRICA
INDIAN OCEAN

Mediterranean Sea
ISRAEL
JORDAN
SPHINX ★Cairo
SAUDI ARABIA
LIBYA
Nile River
EGYPT
Red Sea
SUDAN

But Lehner says the most convincing evidence lies in a temple that was built in front of the statue. Lehner believes that the temple and the Sphinx are part of the same master building plan overseen by one person. Ancient workers built the temple on top of part of another structure that's been proven to be the work of Khafre. Lehner believes that this means the Sphinx and its temple must have been constructed after Khafre's first structure was built—Khufu wouldn't have been around to build on top of Khafre's lower structure. "To me, that's strong evidence that the Sphinx couldn't have been Khufu's," Lehner says.

DISAPPEARING ACT

Today the ancient Egyptians' work is crumbling. Centuries of wind and water have ground away at the Sphinx's limestone, and shifting sands have threatened to cover much of it. Archaeologists work tirelessly to repair the structure to keep it from completely disappearing.

By preserving the Sphinx, experts are also protecting clues that might still be hidden in the statue's stone. Someday, these could be the keys that unlock even more of the Sphinx's secrets.

225

5 COOL THINGS ABOUT ANCIENT GREECE

ALTHOUGH THEY LIVED MORE THAN 2,000 YEARS AGO, the ancient Greeks were clearly ahead of their time. From science to sports, many Greek traditions are alive and well today. Here are some things that make this civilization stand out.

1 START-UP SCHOOL

In 387 B.C., the Greek philosopher Plato founded the Academy in Athens, which was the earliest example of a modern university. Students (including some women, against the traditions of the time) studied astronomy, biology, math, law, politics, and philosophy. Plato's hope was that the Academy would provide a place for all scholars to work toward better government in the Grecian cities. The Academy would become a center of learning for nearly 1,000 years.

2 OUTDOOR STAGE

The Greeks were among the first to perform plays. These performances sprang from festivals honoring their gods in which men would dress up, act out stories, and sing songs. They built large, outdoor theaters in most of their cities—some big enough to hold 15,000 people! The audience was so far away from the stage that the actors would wear elaborate costumes and sad- or happy-face masks so that people could see each character's expressions no matter where they were sitting.

3 CITY-STATES

Experts believe that ancient Greek civilization was likely begun nearly 4,000 years ago by the Mycenaeans of Crete, a Greek island. The ancient Greek Empire spread from Greece through Europe, and in 800 B.C. the Greeks began splitting their land into hundreds of city-states. Although most Greeks shared the same language and religion, each city-state maintained its own laws, customs, and rulers.

4 SUPERSTITIONS

The ancient Greeks were superstitious people. For instance, they originated the idea that breaking a mirror was bad luck. Believing mirrors showed the will of the gods, they thought a broken mirror meant the gods did not want you to see something unpleasant in your future. They also had unique ideas about food—some ancient Greeks would not eat beans because they believed they contained the souls of the dead.

5 ORIGINAL OLYMPICS

The ancient Greeks held many festivals in honor of their gods, including some serious sports competitions. The most famous took place in Olympia, Greece, starting in 776 B.C. Honoring the god Zeus, this two-day event—which inspired the modern-day Olympic Games—included contests in wrestling, boxing, long jump, javelin, discus, and chariot racing. Winners were given a wreath of leaves, free meals, and the best seats in the theater as prizes.

ALEXANDER THE GREAT

A bold military leader, Alexander the Great had a need to lead—and he conquered enough land to create an empire that stretched across 3,000 miles (4,828 km). Get the scoop on the life of this legendary ruler.

Historians think Alexander likely had two different colored eyes—one hazel and one green.

START

ca 356 B.C.

Alexander is born to King Philip II and Queen Olympias, rulers of the ancient Greek kingdom of Macedon. Alexander's tutor is a famous philosopher named Aristotle, who teaches the young prince and his friends about medicine, religion, logic, and art. What, no gym class?

Um—my horse ate my homework?

ca 336 B.C.

Macedon's new king conquers his first city: Thessaly, a neighbor to the south. Alexander and his men sneak up behind Mount Ossa, a nearby mountain range separating the two locations, and surprise the Thessalian guards while they're sleeping. Guess it's true—you snooze, you lose.

ca 338 B.C.

Alexander helps his father command troops at the Battle of Chaeronea (Cair-oh-NEE-ah). He becomes ruler two years later at the age of 20, following King Philip's death.

Historians don't always know the exact dates of events from ancient times. That's why you'll see a "ca" next to the years listed below. It stands for "circa," meaning "around."

ca 331 B.C.

Alexander invades Egypt and takes over the kingdom. The ruler is crowned pharaoh and establishes the famous Egyptian city of Alexandria, naming it after (duh!) himself.

WELCOME TO ALEXANDR

MINE
MINE
MINE

ca 323 B.C.

Alexander gets sick and dies at the age of 32. In just 13 years, he has built a massive empire spreading from Africa to Asia, and introduced Greek culture to much of the world. Now that is pretty great.

GUARDIANS
OF THE TOMB

Back in 1974, some Chinese farmers were digging for water when they got a shock. Staring up from the soil was a face, eyes wide open, with features that looked almost human. But this was not a skeleton: It was one of thousands of life-size soldiers made of baked clay called terra-cotta—and they had been buried for 2,200 years.

BURIED TREASURE

Row upon row of the soldiers—each face as different and as realistic as the next—were hidden in a pit the size of two football fields near Xi'an, which was China's capital city for nearly 2,000 years. Archaeologists eventually found four pits, some containing statues of horse-drawn chariots, cavalry (soldiers on horseback), and high-ranking officers.

BODY GUARDS

Who could have built this huge underground army? Experts assume it was China's first emperor, Qin Shihuangdi (Chin She-hwong-dee). The brilliant but brutal ruler, who created the first unified China, was known for his big ideas and even bigger ego. It's believed that because Qin Shihuangdi had killed so many people during his reign, he may have wanted a large army to protect him from his victims' ghosts once he died. He probably had the clay soldiers created to guard his tomb, which was just one mile (1.6 km) away from where the pits were discovered.

FINAL REWARDS

As it turned out, the emperor's living enemies took revenge—not the dead ones. In 206 B.C., a few years after Qin Shihuangdi's death, invading armies destroyed the pits, burying the warriors and cracking every figure. The pits caved in more as time went on, and the soldiers were lost to the ages.

Experts have since pieced a thousand soldiers back together. But some 6,000 figures are still buried. As work continues, who knows what secrets these soldiers have yet to tell?

STATUES OF ARCHERS, LIKE THE ONE ABOVE, WERE BURIED HOLDING REAL CROSSBOWS.

ANCIENT CRAFTSMEN MADE THOUSANDS OF LIFE-SIZE TERRA-COTTA WARRIORS, EACH WITH A UNIQUE FACE.

UNDER
RECONSTRUCTION

Experts have painstakingly rebuilt and restored a thousand terra-cotta warriors found in underground pits near the emperor's tomb. The complex is so vast that excavations may continue for generations.

A warrior's head poking out of the dirt still has traces of red paint. Originally all of the warriors were painted bright colors.

Workers brush dirt away from the collapsed roof that sheltered the terra-cotta warriors.

A toppled terra-cotta warrior lies in its 2,200-year-old underground tomb.

ASIA

CHINA

PACIFIC OCEAN

TERRA-COTTA WARRIORS

CHINA

HORSE-DRAWN CHARIOT

Secrets of the

SCIENTISTS USE CUTTING-EDGE TECHNOLOGY TO UNCOVER NEW EVIDENCE ABOUT HOW THE SHIP SANK.

Sunday, April 14, 1912: The R.M.S. *Titanic* steams across the North Atlantic Ocean. The 882-foot (269-m)-long passenger ship carries 2,208 people on its maiden voyage from Southampton, England, to New York City, in the United States of America.

Suddenly, a dark shape appears. An iceberg scrapes the ship, and within three hours, the *Titanic* sinks. Almost 1,500 people lose their lives.

Scientists have closely studied the *Titanic*'s wreck on the ocean floor since it was discovered in 1985. National Geographic Explorer-in-Residence James Cameron—director of the movies *Titanic* and *Avatar*—assembled a team of experts to examine the shipwreck anew. Using 3D modeling and state-of-the-art technology, the experts reveal new clues about how the *Titanic* sank.

FLOODING

It might have been possible for the ship to sink more slowly, allowing more people to survive. Many of the ship's portholes were found open—most likely because passengers were airing out their rooms and never closed them. This caused the ship to take on water faster.

Something similar also may have happened in one of the grand lobbies, where a large door was found open. "The size of the door is twice the size of the original iceberg damage," Cameron says. "This would have sped up the sinking of the ship."

BREAKING

As the *Titanic* took on water, the front of the ship, called the bow, sank below the surface, causing the back, or stern, to lift into the air. The great stress broke the ship in half. "When the *Titanic* broke in half and the bow pulled away, the bottom likely remained attached to the back of the ship until it, too, was pulled apart," Cameron says.

EXPLORER JAMES CAMERON PILOTS AN UNDERWATER VEHICLE CALLED A SUBMERSIBLE.

SINKING

In its final resting place, the bow looks remarkably intact. But the stern looks like a bomb destroyed it. Why? The bow was filled with water when it sank, so the pressure was the same on the inside as the outside. The stern, however, sank with lots of air inside and imploded from the pressure.

FINAL IMPACT

The sinking ship created a massive trail of water that followed it downward at 20 to 25 miles an hour (32 to 40 km/h). Experts think that this water trail pummeled the *Titanic* after it hit bottom. "Millions of gallons of water came pushing down on it," Cameron says.

With all this new information, is our understanding of the *Titanic* tragedy complete? "I think we have a very good picture of what happened," Cameron says. "But there will always be mysteries."

Titanic

TITANIC
19 — 12
LONDON

SUPERSIZE SHIP

The *Titanic* was almost as long as three football fields. With its smoke-stacks, the ship was as tall as a 17-story building.

TITANIC

WHAT IF ...

Scientists know a lot about how the *Titanic* sank, but other factors contributed as well.

SAILING SCHEDULE

The *Titanic* set sail more than three weeks behind schedule. If the ship had left on time, an iceberg probably wouldn't have been in its path.

FROM CALM TO CHAOS

The sea was unusually calm on April 14, 1912. Waves would have made the iceberg easier to spot.

MISSED MESSAGES

Two messages were telegraphed from other ships to warn the *Titanic* of icebergs, but they never reached the captain.

We asked oceanographer and National Geographic Explorer-in-Residence Robert Ballard, who led the team that discovered the *Titanic* in 1985, what it felt like to make the discovery of the century.

"My first reaction was one of excitement and celebration. But we were at the **very spot** on the **cold North Atlantic Ocean** where it all happened. So then we had **a quiet moment of remembrance."**

231

THE GREATEST HEISTS OF ALL TIME!

How criminal masterminds pulled off daring thefts—but still got caught.

TRAIN BANDITS

Where: Buckinghamshire, England
Date: August 8, 1963
The Loot: More than £2.6 million ($7 million) in Scottish banknotes from a Royal Mail Train.
The Master Plan: A team of 15 criminals rigs the train signal so the train stops unexpectedly. When it does, they jump into a car filled with mail sacks carrying the money. The thieves transfer the treasure to their vehicle and speed away to their hideout, a farmhouse 27 miles (43 km) away.
The Outcome: A tip leads investigators to the thieves' hideout, where they find stolen mail sacks and fingerprints on everything. Twelve thieves are taken to jail; three are never found.

A DAZZLING CRIME

Where: Antwerp, Belgium
Date: February 16, 2003
The Loot: More than 75 million euros ($100 million) worth of jewels, gold, and money from a vault under the Antwerp World Diamond Centre.
The Master Plan: Thieves spend two and a half years planning the robbery. Using hair spray, tape, and Styrofoam boxes, the thieves block the heat, light, and motion sensors so they can't detect the men's body temperatures or movements. They figure out the combination to the vault's three-ton (2.7-t) steel door by installing a tiny hidden camera.
The Outcome: Police discover a bag in the woods with two of the robbers' DNA. Four of the thieves go to jail. The stolen gems are never recovered.

THE ARTFUL CROOK

Where: Paris, France
Date: August 21, 1911
The Loot: The priceless "Mona Lisa"
The Master Plan: A man named Vincenzo Perugia poses as a workman at the Louvre art museum in Paris, grabs the famous painting, and walks past an unmanned guard station with it tucked under his smock.
The Outcome: After hiding the painting in a wooden trunk for two years, Perugia takes it to an art dealer in Florence, Italy—the same city where the "Mona Lisa" was painted by Leonardo da Vinci about 400 years earlier. The suspicious dealer calls the police, who arrest Perugia and return the "Mona Lisa" to the Louvre.

CURSE OF THE HOPE DIAMOND

Is the Hope Diamond, one of the world's most valuable jewels, the bearer of bad luck? Legend has it that the stone was stolen from the eye of a sacred statue in India, and Hindu gods cursed the stone to punish the thieves. You decide if the curse is rock solid or just a gem of a tale!

LOSING THEIR HEADS

The French royal family once owned the diamond, but not for too long. After King Louis XVI and his wife, Marie Antoinette, were imprisoned and beheaded during the French Revolution, the government confiscated the stone, which thieves later stole before it was bought by the wealthy Hope family.

LOST HOPE

Lord Francis Hope eventually inherited the diamond, and then his wife left him and he had to sell the pricey stone to help pay off his huge debts. But the gem still bears the Hope family name.

TEMPTING FATE

Millionaire Evalyn McLean bought the diamond in 1911. But luck was not on McLean's side, either. During her lifetime, two of her children died, her husband became mentally ill, and she fell into serious debt.

DOOMED DELIVERY

In 1958 a mailman named James Todd delivered the diamond to its present home—the Smithsonian Institution in Washington, D.C., U.S.A. Within a year Todd's wife died and his house burned down. Was it the curse?

REAL OR FAKE?

"The curse isn't true," says Richard Kurin, author of the book *Hope Diamond: The Legendary History of a Cursed Gem*. It may all just be an eerie coincidence, but one thing's for sure, "The Hope diamond is so valuable because it is a unique stone and because of its famous story," says Kurin.

WHERE DO DIAMONDS COME FROM?

Natural diamonds form about 100 miles (160 km) underground and are the hardest known natural substance. Under extreme heat and pressure, carbon atoms are squeezed together into the hard, clear crystals. Volcanic eruptions carry the diamonds toward Earth's surface, where they are mined for use in industrial tools and sparkly jewelry.

GOING TO WAR

Since the beginning of time, different countries, territories, and cultures have feuded with each other over land, power, and politics. Major military conflicts include the following wars:

1095–1291 THE CRUSADES
Starting late in the 11th century, these wars over religion were fought in the Middle East for nearly 200 years.

1337–1453 HUNDRED YEARS' WAR
France and England battled over rights to land for more than a century before the French eventually drove the English out in 1453.

1754–1763 FRENCH AND INDIAN WAR (part of Europe's Seven Years' War)
A nine-year war between the British and French for control of North America.

1775–1783 AMERICAN REVOLUTION
Thirteen British colonies in America united to reject the rule of the British government and to form the United States of America.

1861–1865 AMERICAN CIVIL WAR
Occurred when the northern states (the Union) went to war with the southern states, which had seceded, or withdrawn, to form the Confederate States of America. Slavery was one of the key issues in the Civil War.

1910–1920 MEXICAN REVOLUTION
The people of Mexico revolted against the rule of dictator President Porfirio Díaz, leading to his eventual defeat and to a democratic government.

1914–1918 WORLD WAR I
The assassination of Austria's Archduke Ferdinand by a Serbian nationalist sparked this wide-spreading war. The U.S. entered after Germany sank the British ship *Lusitania,* killing more than 120 Americans.

1918–1920 RUSSIAN CIVIL WAR
Following the 1917 Russian Revolution, this conflict pitted the Communist Red Army against the foreign-backed White Army. The Red Army won, leading to the establishment of the Union of Soviet Socialist Republics (U.S.S.R.) in 1922.

1936–1939 SPANISH CIVIL WAR
Aid from Italy and Germany helped the Nationalists gain victory over the Communist-supported Republicans. The war resulted in the loss of more than 300,000 lives and increased tension in Europe leading up to World War II.

1939–1945 WORLD WAR II
This massive conflict in Europe, Asia, and North Africa involved many countries that aligned with the two sides: the Allies and the Axis. After the bombing of Pearl Harbor in Hawaii in 1941, the U.S. entered the war on the side of the Allies. More than 50 million people died during the war.

1946–1949 CHINESE CIVIL WAR

Also known as the "War of Liberation," this war pitted the Communist and Nationalist Parties in China against each other. The Communists won.

1950–1953 KOREAN WAR

Kicked off when the Communist forces of North Korea, with backing from the Soviet Union, invaded their democratic neighbor to the south. A coalition of 16 countries from the United Nations stepped in to support South Korea. An armistice ended active fighting in 1953.

1950s–1975 VIETNAM WAR

Fought between the Communist North, supported by allies including China, and the government of South Vietnam, supported by the United States and other anticommunist nations.

1967 SIX-DAY WAR

A battle for land between Israel and the states of Egypt, Jordan, and Syria. The outcome resulted in Israel's gaining control of coveted territory, including the Gaza Strip and the West Bank.

1991–PRESENT SOMALI CIVIL WAR

Began when Somalia's last president, a dictator named Mohamed Siad Barre, was overthrown. The war has led to years of fighting and anarchy.

2001–2014 WAR IN AFGHANISTAN

After attacks in the U.S. by the terrorist group al Qaeda, a coalition that eventually included more than 40 countries invaded Afghanistan to find Osama bin Laden and other al Qaeda members and to dismantle the Taliban. Bin Laden was killed in a U.S. covert operation in 2011. The North Atlantic Treaty Organization (NATO) took control of the coalition's combat mission in 2003. That combat mission officially ended in 2014.

2003–2011 WAR IN IRAQ

A coalition led by the U.S., and including Britain, Australia, and Spain, invaded Iraq over suspicions that Iraq had weapons of mass destruction.

Navajo Code Talkers

In 1942, the United States was embroiled in World War II over the South Pacific. The Japanese air attacks had crippled the U.S. Pacific Fleet at Pearl Harbor. To outwit Japanese forces, the U.S. needed a secret way to relay sensitive information, like battle plans and enemy positions—without anyone on the outside catching wind of it.

Enter Philip Johnston, a World War I veteran with a plan. Having grown up on a Navajo reservation, he spoke the Navajo language and pitched it to the U.S. Marines as an uncrackable spoken code. After all, the language was unwritten and known to fewer than 30 non-Navajo people. The Marines agreed to recruit other soldiers to test it out. A crew of 29 Navajo speakers were trained as Code Talkers to communicate in a way that would throw off the Japanese.

But the Code Talkers didn't just speak straight Navajo. When they were talking about important military terms, they'd use Navajo words that loosely translated to the term, like "besh-lo," or iron fish, for submarine and "atsá," or eagle, for transport plane. To the enemy's ears, the communication sounded like a bunch of random syllables strung together, but the Code Talkers understood every word.

The Code Talkers were able to deliver thousands of messages to the battlefields and assist in many major turning points during the war, including the U.S. victory at the Battle of Iwo Jima. By the end of World War II, there were more than 400 Code Talkers working to keep opposing forces in the dark.

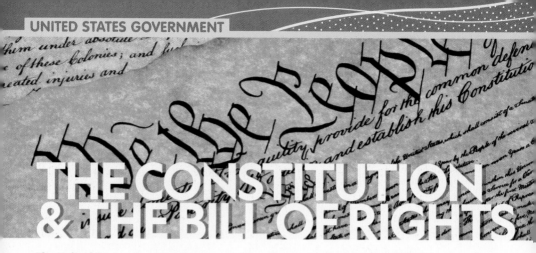

THE CONSTITUTION & THE BILL OF RIGHTS

The United States Constitution was written in 1787 by a group of political leaders from the 13 states that made up the U.S. at the time. Thirty-nine men, including Benjamin Franklin and James Madison, signed the document to create a national government. While some feared the creation of a strong federal government, all 13 states eventually ratified, or approved, the Constitution, making it the law of the land. The Constitution has three major parts: the preamble, the articles, and the amendments.

Here's a summary of what topics are covered in each part of the Constitution. Check out the Constitution online or at your local library for the full text.

THE PREAMBLE outlines the basic purposes of the government: *We the People of the United States, in order to form a more perfect Union, establish justice, insure domestic tranquility, provide for the common defense, promote the general welfare, and secure the blessings of liberty to ourselves and our posterity, do ordain and establish this Constitution for the United States of America.*

SEVEN ARTICLES outline the powers of Congress, the president, and the court system:

Article I outlines the legislative branch—the Senate and the House of Representatives—and its powers and responsibilities.

Article II outlines the executive branch—the presidency—and its powers and responsibilities.

Article III outlines the judicial branch—the court system—and its powers and responsibilities.

Article IV describes the individual states' rights and powers.

Article V outlines the amendment process.

Article VI establishes the Constitution as the law of the land.

Article VII gives the requirements for the Constitution to be approved.

THE AMENDMENTS, or additions to the Constitution, were put in later as needed. In 1791, the first 10 amendments, known as the **Bill of Rights,** were added. Since then, another 17 amendments have been added. This is the Bill of Rights:

1st Amendment: guarantees freedom of religion, speech, and the press, and the right to assemble and petition. The U.S. may not have a national religion.

2nd Amendment: discusses the militia and the right of people to bear arms

3rd Amendment: prohibits the military or troops from using private homes without consent

4th Amendment: protects people and their homes from search, arrest, or seizure without probable cause or a warrant

5th Amendment: grants people the right to have a trial and prevents punishment before prosecution; protects private property from being taken without compensation

6th Amendment: guarantees the right to a speedy and public trial

7th Amendment: guarantees a trial by jury in certain cases

8th Amendment: forbids "cruel and unusual punishments"

9th Amendment: states that the Constitution is not all-encompassing and does not deny people other, unspecified rights

10th Amendment: grants the powers not covered by the Constitution to the states and the people

Read the full text version of the United States Constitution at constitutioncenter.org/constitution/full-text

White House

BRANCHES OF GOVERNMENT

The **UNITED STATES GOVERNMENT** is divided into three branches: executive, legislative, and judicial. The system of checks and balances is a way to control power and to make sure one branch can't take the reins of government. For example, most of the president's actions require the approval of Congress. Likewise, the laws passed in Congress must be signed by the president before they can take effect.

Executive Branch

The Constitution lists the central powers of the president: to serve as commander in chief of the armed forces; make treaties with other nations; grant pardons; inform Congress on the state of the union; and appoint ambassadors, officials, and judges. The executive branch includes the president and the 15 governmental departments.

Legislative Branch

This branch is made up of Congress—the Senate and the House of Representatives. The Constitution grants Congress the power to make laws. Congress is made up of elected representatives from each state. Each state has two representatives in the Senate, while the number of representatives in the House is determined by the size of the state's population. Washington, D.C., and the territories elect nonvoting representatives to the House of Representatives. The Founding Fathers set up this system as a compromise between big states—which wanted representation based on population—and small states—which wanted all states to have equal representation rights.

The U.S. Capitol in Washington, D.C.

Judicial Branch

The U.S. Supreme Court Building in Washington, D.C.

The judicial branch is composed of the federal court system—the U.S. Supreme Court, the courts of appeals, and the district courts. The Supreme Court is the most powerful court. Its motto is "Equal Justice Under Law." This influential court is responsible for interpreting the Constitution and applying it to the cases that it hears. The decisions of the Supreme Court are absolute—they are the final word on any legal question.

There are nine justices on the Supreme Court. They are appointed by the president of the United States and confirmed by the Senate.

237

The American Indian Experience

American Indians are indigenous to North and South America—they are the people who were here before Columbus and other European explorers came to these lands. They lived in nations, tribes, and bands across both continents. For decades following the arrival of Europeans in 1492, American Indians clashed with the newcomers who had ruptured the Indians' ways of living.

Tribal Land

During the 19th century, both United States legislation and military action restricted the movement of American Indians, forcing them to live on reservations and attempting to dismantle tribal structures. For centuries, Indians were displaced or killed, or became assimilated into the general U.S. population. In 1924 the Indian Citizenship Act granted citizenship to all American Indians. Unfortunately, this was not enough to end the social discrimination and mistreatment that many Indians have faced. Today, American Indians living in the U.S. still face many challenges.

Healing the Past

Many members of the 560-plus recognized tribes in the United States live primarily on reservations. Some tribes have more than one reservation, while others have none. Together these reservations make up less than 3 percent of the nation's land area. The tribal governments on reservations have the right to form their own governments and to enforce laws, similar to individual states. Many feel that this sovereignty is still not enough to right the wrongs of the past: They hope for a change in the U.S. government's relationship with American Indians.

Arizona, California, and Oklahoma have the largest American Indian populations by state.

American Indians invented kayaks, snowshoes, and lacrosse.

Top: A Cherokee and Catawba man dances at a powwow.
Middle: A Monacan girl dances in a traditional jingle dress.
Bottom: Little Shell men in traditional costume

The president of the United States is the chief of the executive branch, the commander in chief of the U.S. armed forces, and head of the federal government. Elected every four years, the president is the highest policy-maker in the nation. The 22nd Amendment (1951) says that no person may be elected to the office of president more than twice. There have been 45 presidencies and 44 presidents.

JAMES MONROE
5th President of the United States ★ 1817–1825

BORN April 28, 1758, in Westmoreland County, VA

POLITICAL PARTY Democratic-Republican

NO. OF TERMS two

VICE PRESIDENT Daniel D. Tompkins

DIED July 4, 1831, in New York, NY

GEORGE WASHINGTON
1st President of the United States ★ 1789–1797

BORN Feb. 22, 1732, in Pope's Creek, Westmoreland County, VA

POLITICAL PARTY Federalist

NO. OF TERMS two

VICE PRESIDENT John Adams

DIED Dec. 14, 1799, at Mount Vernon, VA

MONROVIA, the capital of the African country Liberia, is named after JAMES MONROE.

Monrovia

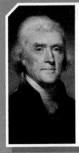

JOHN ADAMS
2nd President of the United States ★ 1797–1801

BORN Oct. 30, 1735, in Braintree (now Quincy), MA

POLITICAL PARTY Federalist

NO. OF TERMS one

VICE PRESIDENT Thomas Jefferson

DIED July 4, 1826, in Quincy, MA

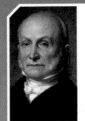

JOHN QUINCY ADAMS
6th President of the United States ★ 1825–1829

BORN July 11, 1767, in Braintree (now Quincy), MA

POLITICAL PARTY Democratic-Republican

NO. OF TERMS one

VICE PRESIDENT John Caldwell Calhoun

DIED Feb. 23, 1848, at the U.S. Capitol, Washington, D.C.

THOMAS JEFFERSON
3rd President of the United States ★ 1801–1809

BORN April 13, 1743, at Shadwell, Goochland (now Albemarle) County, VA

POLITICAL PARTY Democratic-Republican

NO. OF TERMS two

VICE PRESIDENTS 1st term: Aaron Burr
2nd term: George Clinton

DIED July 4, 1826, at Monticello, Charlottesville, VA

ANDREW JACKSON
7th President of the United States ★ 1829–1837

BORN March 15, 1767, in the Waxhaw region, NC and SC

POLITICAL PARTY Democrat

NO. OF TERMS two

VICE PRESIDENTS 1st term: John Caldwell Calhoun
2nd term: Martin Van Buren

DIED June 8, 1845, in Nashville, TN

JAMES MADISON
4th President of the United States ★ 1809–1817

BORN March 16, 1751, at Belle Grove, Port Conway, VA

POLITICAL PARTY Democratic-Republican

NO. OF TERMS two

VICE PRESIDENTS 1st term: George Clinton
2nd term: Elbridge Gerry

DIED June 28, 1836, at Montpelier, Orange County, VA

MARTIN VAN BUREN
8th President of the United States ★ 1837–1841

BORN Dec. 5, 1782, in Kinderhook, NY

POLITICAL PARTY Democrat

NO. OF TERMS one

VICE PRESIDENT Richard M. Johnson

DIED July 24, 1862, in Kinderhook, NY

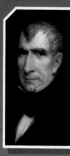

WILLIAM HENRY HARRISON

9th President of the United States ★ *1841*

BORN Feb. 9, 1773, in Charles City County, VA

POLITICAL PARTY Whig

NO. OF TERMS one (cut short by death)

VICE PRESIDENT John Tyler

DIED April 4, 1841, in the White House, Washington, D.C.

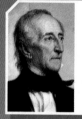

JOHN TYLER

10th President of the United States ★ *1841–1845*

BORN March 29, 1790, in Charles City County, VA

POLITICAL PARTY Whig

NO. OF TERMS one (partial)

VICE PRESIDENT none

DIED Jan. 18, 1862, in Richmond, VA

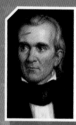

JAMES K. POLK

11th President of the United States ★ *1845–1849*

BORN Nov. 2, 1795, near Pineville, Mecklenburg County, NC

POLITICAL PARTY Democrat

NO. OF TERMS one

VICE PRESIDENT George Mifflin Dallas

DIED June 15, 1849, in Nashville, TN

ZACHARY TAYLOR

12th President of the United States ★ *1849–1850*

BORN Nov. 24, 1784, in Orange County, VA

POLITICAL PARTY Whig

NO. OF TERMS one (cut short by death)

VICE PRESIDENT Millard Fillmore

DIED July 9, 1850, in the White House, Washington, D.C.

MILLARD FILLMORE

13th President of the United States ★ *1850–1853*

BORN Jan. 7, 1800, in Cayuga County, NY

POLITICAL PARTY Whig

NO. OF TERMS one (partial)

VICE PRESIDENT none

DIED March 8, 1874, in Buffalo, NY

FRANKLIN PIERCE

14th President of the United States ★ *1853–1857*

BORN Nov. 23, 1804, in Hillsborough (now Hillsboro), NH

POLITICAL PARTY Democrat

NO. OF TERMS one

VICE PRESIDENT William Rufus De Vane King

DIED Oct. 8, 1869, in Concord, NH

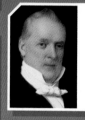

JAMES BUCHANAN

15th President of the United States ★ *1857–1861*

BORN April 23, 1791, in Cove Gap, PA

POLITICAL PARTY Democrat

NO. OF TERMS one

VICE PRESIDENT John Cabell Breckinridge

DIED June 1, 1868, in Lancaster, PA

ABRAHAM LINCOLN

16th President of the United States ★ *1861–1865*

BORN Feb. 12, 1809, near Hodgenville, KY

POLITICAL PARTY Republican (formerly Whig)

NO. OF TERMS two (assassinated)

VICE PRESIDENTS 1st term: Hannibal Hamlin
2nd term: Andrew Johnson

DIED April 15, 1865, in Washington, D.C.

ANDREW JOHNSON

17th President of the United States ★ *1865–1869*

BORN Dec. 29, 1808, in Raleigh, NC

POLITICAL PARTY Democrat

NO. OF TERMS one (partial)

VICE PRESIDENT none

DIED July 31, 1875, in Carter's Station, TN

Before becoming a politician, ANDREW JOHNSON was a TAILOR.

ULYSSES S. GRANT

18th President of the United States ★ 1869–1877

BORN April 27, 1822,
in Point Pleasant, OH

POLITICAL PARTY Republican

NO. OF TERMS two

VICE PRESIDENTS 1st term: Schuyler Colfax
2nd term: Henry Wilson

DIED July 23, 1885, in Mount
McGregor, NY

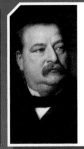

GROVER CLEVELAND

*22nd and 24th President of the United States
1885–1889 ★ 1893–1897*

BORN March 18, 1837, in Caldwell, NJ

POLITICAL PARTY Democrat

NO. OF TERMS two (nonconsecutive)

VICE PRESIDENTS 1st administration:
Thomas Andrews Hendricks
2nd administration:
Adlai Ewing Stevenson

DIED June 24, 1908, in Princeton, NJ

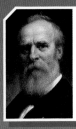

RUTHERFORD B. HAYES

19th President of the United States ★ 1877–1881

BORN Oct. 4, 1822,
in Delaware, OH

POLITICAL PARTY Republican

NO. OF TERMS one

VICE PRESIDENT William Almon Wheeler

DIED Jan. 17, 1893, in Fremont, OH

BENJAMIN HARRISON

23rd President of the United States ★ 1889–1893

BORN Aug. 20, 1833, in North Bend, OH

POLITICAL PARTY Republican

NO. OF TERMS one

VICE PRESIDENT Levi Parsons Morton

DIED March 13, 1901, in Indianapolis, IN

President Rutherford B. Hayes's wife, Lucy, loved pets. The couple owned the **FIRST SIAMESE CAT IN THE COUNTRY.**

WILLIAM MCKINLEY

25th President of the United States ★ 1897–1901

BORN Jan. 29, 1843, in Niles, OH

POLITICAL PARTY Republican

NO. OF TERMS two (assassinated)

VICE PRESIDENTS 1st term:
Garret Augustus Hobart
2nd term:
Theodore Roosevelt

DIED Sept. 14, 1901, in Buffalo, NY

JAMES A. GARFIELD

20th President of the United States ★ 1881

BORN Nov. 19, 1831, near
Orange, OH

POLITICAL PARTY Republican

NO. OF TERMS one (assassinated)

VICE PRESIDENT Chester A. Arthur

DIED Sept. 19, 1881, in Elberon, NJ

THEODORE ROOSEVELT

26th President of the United States ★ 1901–1909

BORN Oct. 27, 1858, in New York, NY

POLITICAL PARTY Republican

NO. OF TERMS one, plus balance of
McKinley's term

VICE PRESIDENTS 1st term: none
2nd term: Charles
Warren Fairbanks

DIED Jan. 6, 1919, in Oyster Bay, NY

CHESTER A. ARTHUR

21st President of the United States ★ 1881–1885

BORN Oct. 5, 1829, in Fairfield, VT

POLITICAL PARTY Republican

NO. OF TERMS one (partial)

VICE PRESIDENT none

DIED Nov. 18, 1886, in New York, NY

WILLIAM HOWARD TAFT

27th President of the United States ★ 1909–1913

BORN Sept. 15, 1857, in Cincinnati, OH

POLITICAL PARTY Republican

NO. OF TERMS one

VICE PRESIDENT James Schoolcraft
Sherman

DIED March 8, 1930, in Washington, D.C.

WOODROW WILSON
28th President of the United States ★ 1913–1921
BORN Dec. 29, 1856, in Staunton, VA
POLITICAL PARTY Democrat
NO. OF TERMS two
VICE PRESIDENT Thomas Riley Marshall
DIED Feb. 3, 1924, in Washington, D.C.

WARREN G. HARDING
29th President of the United States ★ 1921–1923
BORN Nov. 2, 1865, in Caledonia
(now Blooming Grove), OH
POLITICAL PARTY Republican
NO. OF TERMS one (died while in office)
VICE PRESIDENT Calvin Coolidge
DIED Aug. 2, 1923, in San Francisco, CA

CALVIN COOLIDGE
30th President of the United States ★ 1923–1929
BORN July 4, 1872, in Plymouth, VT
POLITICAL PARTY Republican
NO. OF TERMS one, plus balance of
Harding's term
VICE PRESIDENTS 1st term: none
2nd term:
Charles Gates Dawes
DIED Jan. 5, 1933, in Northampton, MA

HERBERT HOOVER
31st President of the United States ★ 1929–1933
BORN Aug. 10, 1874,
in West Branch, IA
POLITICAL PARTY Republican
NO. OF TERMS one
VICE PRESIDENT Charles Curtis
DIED Oct. 20, 1964, in New York, NY

FRANKLIN D. ROOSEVELT
32nd President of the United States ★ 1933–1945
BORN Jan. 30, 1882, in Hyde Park, NY
POLITICAL PARTY Democrat
NO. OF TERMS four (died while in office)
VICE PRESIDENTS 1st & 2nd terms: John
Nance Garner; 3rd term:
Henry Agard Wallace;
4th term: Harry S. Truman
DIED April 12, 1945,
in Warm Springs, GA

HARRY S. TRUMAN
33rd President of the United States ★ 1945–1953
BORN May 8, 1884, in Lamar, MO
POLITICAL PARTY Democrat
NO. OF TERMS one, plus balance of
Franklin D. Roosevelt's term
VICE PRESIDENTS 1st term: none
2nd term:
Alben William Barkley
DIED Dec. 26, 1972, in Independence, MO

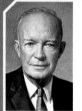

DWIGHT D. EISENHOWER
34th President of the United States ★ 1953–1961
BORN Oct. 14, 1890, in Denison, TX
POLITICAL PARTY Republican
NO. OF TERMS two
VICE PRESIDENT Richard Nixon
DIED March 28, 1969,
in Washington, D.C.

JOHN F. KENNEDY
35th President of the United States ★ 1961–1963
BORN May 29, 1917, in Brookline, MA
POLITICAL PARTY Democrat
NO. OF TERMS one (assassinated)
VICE PRESIDENT Lyndon B. Johnson
DIED Nov. 22, 1963, in Dallas, TX

LYNDON B. JOHNSON
36th President of the United States ★ 1963–1969
BORN Aug. 27, 1908, near Stonewall, TX
POLITICAL PARTY Democrat
NO. OF TERMS one, plus balance of
Kennedy's term
VICE PRESIDENTS 1st term: none
2nd term: Hubert
Horatio Humphrey
DIED Jan. 22, 1973, near San Antonio, TX

Lyndon B. Johnson's beagles were named HIM and HER..

RICHARD NIXON

37th President of the United States ★ 1969–1974

BORN Jan. 9, 1913, in Yorba Linda, CA
POLITICAL PARTY Republican
NO. OF TERMS two (resigned)
VICE PRESIDENTS 1st term & 2nd term (partial): Spiro Theodore Agnew; 2nd term (balance): Gerald R. Ford
DIED April 22, 1994, in New York, NY

GERALD R. FORD

38th President of the United States ★ 1974–1977

BORN July 14, 1913, in Omaha, NE
POLITICAL PARTY Republican
NO. OF TERMS one (partial)
VICE PRESIDENT Nelson Aldrich Rockefeller
DIED Dec. 26, 2006, in Rancho Mirage, CA

JIMMY CARTER

39th President of the United States ★ 1977–1981

BORN Oct. 1, 1924, in Plains, GA
POLITICAL PARTY Democrat
NO. OF TERMS one
VICE PRESIDENT Walter Frederick (Fritz) Mondale

RONALD REAGAN

40th President of the United States ★ 1981–1989

BORN Feb. 6, 1911, in Tampico, IL
POLITICAL PARTY Republican
NO. OF TERMS two
VICE PRESIDENT George H. W. Bush
DIED June 5, 2004, in Los Angeles, CA

GEORGE H. W. BUSH

41st President of the United States ★ 1989–1993

BORN June 12, 1924, in Milton, MA
POLITICAL PARTY Republican
NO. OF TERMS one
VICE PRESIDENT James Danforth (Dan) Quayle III
DIED November 30, 2018, in Houston, TX

BILL CLINTON

42nd President of the United States ★ 1993–2001

BORN Aug. 19, 1946, in Hope, AR
POLITICAL PARTY Democrat
NO. OF TERMS two
VICE PRESIDENT Albert Arnold Gore, Jr.

GEORGE W. BUSH

43rd President of the United States ★ 2001–2009

BORN July 6, 1946, in New Haven, CT
POLITICAL PARTY Republican
NO. OF TERMS two
VICE PRESIDENT Richard Bruce Cheney

BARACK OBAMA

44th President of the United States ★ 2009–2017

BORN Aug. 4, 1961, in Honolulu, HI
POLITICAL PARTY Democrat
NO. OF TERMS two
VICE PRESIDENT Joseph R. Biden, Jr.

To avoid germs, Donald J. Trump prefers HIGH FIVES to HANDSHAKES.

DONALD TRUMP

45th President of the United States ★ 2017–present

BORN June 14, 1946, in Queens, NY
POLITICAL PARTY Republican
VICE PRESIDENT Mike Pence

PRANKSTERS IN CHIEF
Real-life practical jokes played by U.S. presidents

The job of president of the United States is a stressful one. But even the most serious commanders in chief had fun while working in the White House. Check out seven of the best pranks ever pulled by U.S. presidents.

BARRY FUNNY

Barack Obama is best known as the 44th president of the United States—not as "Barry," a childhood nickname. But the former president dusted off his old title in 2009 to prank call then Virginia governor Tim Kaine. Kaine was being interviewed on a radio show when Obama dialed in to pose as a regular local citizen, Barry in D.C. The in-disguise president quickly revealed his true identity, then thanked the good-natured Kaine for his service to the state of Virginia.

LOST LETTERS

In 2001, incoming president George W. Bush's staff faced an unexpected problem: They couldn't type Bush's full name! That's because pranksters working for the previous president, Bill Clinton, had pried the W's from dozens of keyboards across the White House complex.

COPYCAT IN CHIEF

Before President Abraham Lincoln was known as the "Great Emancipator" for freeing the slaves during the Civil War of 1861 to 1865, he earned a reputation as a great imitator. In 1840, Lincoln mimicked the mannerisms of political rival Jesse Thomas so well that he had the audience cracking up. His impersonation was talked about for years afterward.

HIDE AND SNEAK

The job of president comes with many perks—including the ability to summon Secret Service agents at the push of a button. President Calvin Coolidge reportedly liked this power a little too much when he was in office from 1923 to 1929. He would supposedly call in his security detail to the Oval Office, then hide under his desk as his employees searched the office for the man they were sworn to protect.

BIG SHOT

When reporter Tony Vaccaro was told he might need an immunization shot to travel with President Harry S. Truman to South America in 1947, he wasn't happy—especially when Vaccaro saw the giant needle. That's when a man burst into the room and said, "This won't hurt a bit, Tony." It was President Truman, who had learned of Vaccaro's fear of needles and decided to make the reporter sweat.

WATER LANDING

President Lyndon B. Johnson, who served from 1963 to 1969, loved to collect vehicles. One of his favorites was a blue convertible that he kept at his Texas ranch. But disaster always seemed to strike as he and his guests sped down a hill toward a lake. "The brakes don't work—we're going in!" he'd yell as the car hit the water. But just as his passengers tried to escape, President Johnson would laugh. The convertible was actually an Amphicar, a vehicle that looked like a car ... but could float like a boat!

UP AND AWAY

President Franklin D. Roosevelt, who was in office from 1933 to 1945, once told a Secret Service agent to climb on the roof of a farm building to fetch something. But Roosevelt didn't stick around for the agent to climb down. The president had the ladder removed and drove away, leaving the agent (temporarily) stranded.

CIVIL RIGHTS

Although the Constitution protects the civil rights of American citizens, it has not always been able to protect all Americans from persecution or discrimination. During the first half of the 20th century, many Americans, particularly African Americans, were subjected to widespread discrimination and racism. By the mid-1950s, many people were eager to end the bonds of racism and bring freedom to all men and women.

The civil rights movement of the 1950s and 1960s sought to end racial discrimination against African Americans, especially in the southern states. The movement wanted to restore the fundamentals of economic and social equality to those who had been oppressed.

Woolworth Counter Sit-in

On February 1, 1960, four African-American college students strolled into a Woolworth's "five-and-dime" store in Greensboro, North Carolina. They planned to have lunch there, but were refused service as soon as they sat down at the counter. In a time of heightened racial tension, the Woolworth's manager had a strict whites-only policy. But the students wouldn't take no for an answer. The men—later dubbed the "Greensboro Four"—stayed seated, peacefully and quietly, at the lunch counter until closing. The next day, they returned with 15 additional college students. The following day, even more. By February 5, some 300 students gathered at Woolworth's, forming one of the most famous sit-ins of the civil rights movement. The protest—which sparked similar sit-ins throughout the country—worked: Just six months later, restaurants across the south began to integrate.

Key Events in the Civil Rights Movement

1954	The Supreme Court case *Brown* v. *Board of Education* declares school segregation illegal.
1955	Rosa Parks refuses to give up her bus seat to a white passenger and spurs a bus boycott.
1957	The Little Rock Nine help to integrate schools.
1960	Four black college students begin sit-ins at a restaurant in Greensboro, North Carolina.
1961	Freedom Rides to southern states begin as a way to protest segregation in transportation.
1963	Martin Luther King, Jr., leads the famous March on Washington.
1964	The Civil Rights Act, signed by President Lyndon B. Johnson, prohibits discrimination based on race, color, religion, sex, and national origin.
1967	Thurgood Marshall becomes the first African American to be named to the Supreme Court.
1968	President Lyndon B. Johnson signs the Civil Rights Act of 1968, which prohibits discrimination in the sale, rental, and financing of housing.

STONE OF HOPE:
THE LEGACY OF MARTIN LUTHER KING, JR.

On April 4, 1968, Dr. Martin Luther King, Jr., was shot by James Earl Ray while standing on a hotel balcony in Memphis, Tennessee. The news of his death sent shock waves throughout the world: Dr. King, a Baptist minister and founder of the Southern Christian Leadership Conference (SCLC), was the most prominent civil rights leader of his time. His nonviolent protests and marches against segregation, as well as his powerful speeches—including his famous "I Have a Dream" speech—motivated people to fight for justice for all.

More than 50 years after his death, Dr. King's dream lives on through a memorial on the National Mall in Washington, D.C. Built in 2011, the memorial features a 30-foot (9-m) statue of Dr. King carved into a granite boulder named the "Stone of Hope."

Today, Dr. King continues to inspire people around the world with his words and his vision for a peaceful world without racism. He will forever be remembered as one of the most prominent leaders of the civil rights movement.

"The time is always right to do what is right."

Martin Luther King, Jr. Memorial in Washington, D.C.

The Smithsonian's National Museum of African American History and Culture in Washington, D.C., is filled with powerful artifacts, including stools from the Woolworth's lunch counter in Greensboro, North Carolina, and a dress Rosa Parks was making the day she was famously arrested for refusing to give up her bus seat for a white person.

Rosa Parks

The average person spends six hours at the Museum of African American History—compared to two hours at other museums.

247

WOMEN

FIGHTING FOR EQUALITY

Women in New York City cast their votes for the first time in November 1920.

Today, women make up about half of the country's workforce. But a little over a century ago, less than 20 percent worked outside the home. In fact, they didn't even have the right to vote!

That began to change in the mid-1800s when women, led by pioneers like Elizabeth Cady Stanton and Susan B. Anthony, started speaking up about inequality. They organized public demonstrations, gave speeches, published documents, and wrote newspaper articles to express their ideas. In 1848, about 300 people attended the Seneca Falls Convention in New York State to address the need for equal rights. By the late 1800s, the National American Woman Suffrage Association had made great strides toward giving women the freedom to vote. One by one, states began allowing women to vote. By 1920, the U.S. Constitution was amended, giving women across the country the ability to cast a vote during any election.

But the fight for equality did not end there. In the 1960s and 1970s, the women's rights movement experienced a rebirth, as feminists protested against injustices in areas such as the workplace and in education.

While these efforts enabled women to make great strides in our society, the efforts to even the playing field among men and women continue today.

New Zealand gave women the right to vote in 1893, becoming the world's first country to do so.

In 2018, Saudi Arabia allowed women to drive for the first time.

Women's March in Boston, Massachusetts, on January 21, 2017

Key Events in Women's History

1848: **Elizabeth Cady Stanton** and **Lucretia Mott** organize the Seneca Falls Convention in New York. Attendees rally for equitable laws, equal educational and job opportunities, and the right to vote.

1920: The 19th Amendment, guaranteeing women the right to vote, is ratified.

1964: Title VII of the Civil Rights Act of 1964, which prohibits employment discrimination on the basis of sex, is successfully amended.

1971: Gloria Steinem heads up the National Women's Political Caucus, which encourages women to be active in government. She also launches *Ms.,* a magazine about women's issues.

1972: Congress approves **the Equal Rights Amendment** (ERA), proposing that women and men have equal rights under the law. It is ratified by 35 of the necessary 38 states, and is still not part of the U.S. Constitution.

1981: President Ronald Reagan appoints **Sandra Day O'Connor** as the first female Supreme Court justice.

2009: President Obama signs **the Lilly Ledbetter Fair Pay Act** to protect against pay discrimination among men and women.

2013: The **ban against women in military combat** positions is removed, overturning a 1994 Pentagon decision restricting women from combat roles.

2016: Democratic presidential nominee **Hillary Rodham Clinton** becomes the first woman to lead the ticket of a major U.S. party.

2017: A crowd of some four million people turned out for the first-ever **Women's March,** a protest advocating women's rights. Events were held in locations throughout the country.

Ruth Bader Ginsburg Rises to the Top

Soft-spoken and small in stature, Ruth Bader Ginsburg's relentless ambition has allowed her to shine as a justice of the United States Supreme Court. Throughout her career, she has broken boundaries by working tirelessly to fight for equal pay for women and was instrumental in changing laws throughout America to favor gender equality. She has also played a role in a ruling that allowed women into the Virginia Military Institute for the first time in the school's 158-year history. Bader Ginsburg will be forever remembered for her contributions to make the world an equal place for everyone.

Maria Mitchell Shoots for the Stars

On a clear evening in October 1847, Maria Mitchell, a 29-year-old librarian from Nantucket, Massachusetts, sat atop the roof of the bank where her father worked as a cashier. A budding astronomer, Mitchell often watched the night skies through the lens of a telescope. That night, a small blurry object caught her eye. It was a comet—previously uncharted by scientists. Now known as Miss Mitchell's Comet, the discovery rocketed Mitchell into the forefront of the astronomy world. She received a gold medal from the king of Denmark, became the first professional female astronomer in the United States, and traveled throughout the country and Europe. Mitchell later went on to have a successful career as a professor of astronomy at Vassar College in New York, where she continued to make discoveries among the stars—and inspired hundreds of students to do the same.

249

QUIZ WHIZ

Go back in time to seek the answers to this history quiz!

Write your answers on a piece of paper. Then check them below.

1 **True or false?** Ancient Egyptians believed that sphinxes could ward off evil.

2 Including its smokestacks, the R.M.S. *Titanic* was as tall as a _____-story building.
a. 5
b. 30
c. 100
d. 17

3 Bandits in England once stole how much from a Royal Mail Train?
a. $1.7 million
b. $7 million
c. $17 million
d. $170 million

MAIL

4 **True or false?** Volcanic eruptions help carry diamonds formed underground to Earth's surface.

5 Some ancient Greeks did not eat beans because they believed they contained _____.
a. methane gas
b. the souls of the dead
c. magical powers
d. poison

Not **STUMPED** yet? Check out the *NATIONAL GEOGRAPHIC KIDS QUIZ WHIZ* collection for more crazy **HISTORY** questions!

ANSWERS: 1. True ; 2. d ; 3. b; 4. True; 5. b

HOMEWORK HELP

Brilliant Biographies

Malala Yousafzai

A biography is the story of a person's life. It can be a brief summary or a long book. Biographers—those who write biographies—use many different sources to learn about their subjects. You can write your own biography of a famous person you find inspiring.

How to Get Started

Choose a subject you find interesting. If you think Cleopatra is cool, you have a good chance of getting your reader interested, too. If you're bored by ancient Egypt, your reader will be snoring after your first paragraph.

Your subject can be almost anyone: an author, an inventor, a celebrity, a politician, or a member of your family. To find someone to write about, ask yourself these simple questions:

1. Who do I want to know more about?
2. What did this person do that was special?
3. How did this person change the world?

Do Your Research

- Find out as much about your subject as possible. Read books, news articles, and encyclopedia entries. Watch video clips and movies, and search the internet. Conduct interviews, if possible.
- Take notes, writing down important facts and interesting stories about your subject.

Write the Biography

- Come up with a title. Include the person's name.
- Write an introduction. Consider asking a probing question about your subject.
- Include information about the person's childhood. When was this person born? Where did he or she grow up? Who did he or she admire?
- Highlight the person's talents, accomplishments, and personal attributes.
- Describe the specific events that helped to shape this person's life. Did this person ever have a problem and overcome it?
- Write a conclusion. Include your thoughts about why it is important to learn about this person.
- Once you have finished your first draft, revise and then proofread your work.

Here's a **SAMPLE BIOGRAPHY** of Malala Yousafzai, a human rights advocate and the youngest ever recipient of the Nobel Peace Prize. Of course, there is so much more for you to discover and write about on your own!

Malala Yousafzai

Malala Yousafzai was born in Pakistan on July 12, 1997. Malala's father, Ziauddin, a teacher, made it his priority for his daughter to receive a proper education. Malala loved school. She learned to speak three different languages and even wrote a blog about her experiences as a student.

Around the time Malala turned 10, the Taliban—a group of strict Muslims who believe women are to stay at home—took over the region where she lived. The Taliban did not approve of Malala's outspoken love of learning. One day, on her way home from school, Malala was shot in the head by a Taliban gunman. Very badly injured, she was sent to a hospital in England.

Not only did Malala survive the shooting—she thrived. She used her experience as a platform to fight for girls' education worldwide. She began speaking out about educational opportunities for all. Her efforts gained worldwide attention and eventually, she was awarded the Nobel Peace Prize in 2014 at the age of 17. She is the youngest person to earn the prestigious prize.

Each year on July 12, World Malala Day honors her heroic efforts to bring attention to human rights issues.

The all-natural rock rainbows of the Zhangye Danxia National Geological Park in north-central China took millions of years to form.

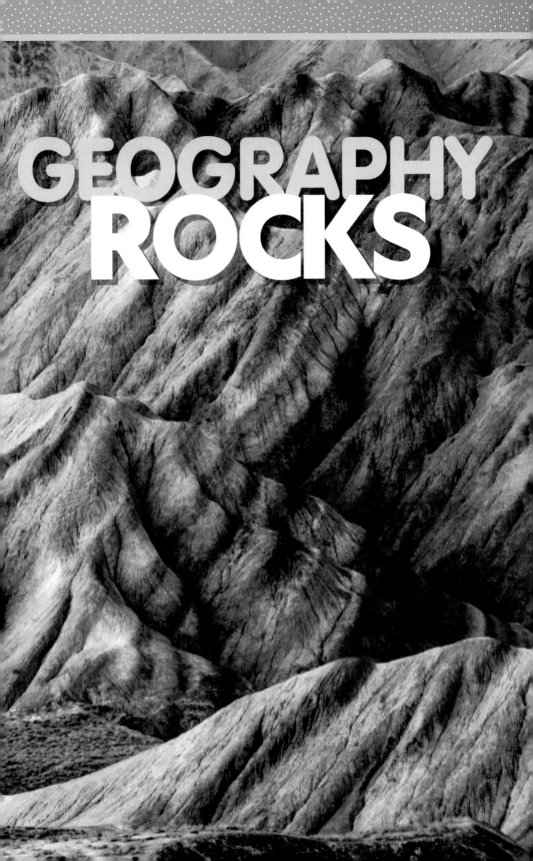

GEOGRAPHY
ROCKS

EARTH EXPLORER
Meet **Alex Tait!**

How National Geographic's Geographer put his passion on the map.

When an iceberg the size of Delaware recently sheared off the Antarctic Peninsula, Alex Tait was watching—and waiting. As the Geographer at National Geographic, Alex keeps the maps up to date. So as the giant iceberg, one of the world's largest, broke away and essentially changed the shape of the continent, Alex took note.

Updating National Geographic's maps of Antarctica to reflect the fractured ice shelf is just one of many jobs Alex tackles in his position. He also monitors other shifts in the world, like boundary changes; creates custom maps; updates existing maps; and makes sure that there's consistency among all of the many maps published in National Geographic's books and magazines, and on its website.

"Maps tell us stories and give us an easier way to understand and care about our world," says Alex.

Alex fell in love with geography as a kid while poring over paper maps as he planned hiking trips with his dad. While technology has changed the way many of us view maps today, Alex believes that the beauty of geography remains the same, whether maps are on a screen or folded out in front of you.

And as technology continues to advance, so will our access to see places from around the globe, says Alex. Want to see the top of Mount Everest? You may one day soon be able to get live images of the famous summit and other far-flung places around the planet.

"Geographic data is getting so comprehensive and maps are getting more and more realistic," says Alex. "And with virtual reality (VR) and augmented reality (AR), you will be able to use a map to go anywhere you want—from the tops of mountains to the bottom of the ocean. Maps literally change the way we view the world."

A person who makes and studies maps is called a cartographer.

A MAP OF MOUNT WASHINGTON IN NEW HAMPSHIRE, U.S.A., THAT ALEX WORKED ON

" Maps are tools to show changes happening on our planet. We recently made a map showing the impact of human activity on the planet, like fishing, shipping, and climate change. "

The earliest maps were drawn on clay tablets some 3,500 years ago.

CALL TO ACTION!

Want to get into geography? It all starts with learning to understand and read maps—and even making some of your own. Whether you use a paper and pencil to draw out the boundaries of your backyard or create a map on your computer, Alex says that making and studying maps will help you get a stronger grip on geography. "I still make my own maps sometimes," says Alex. "Understanding maps is like learning a language. The more you do it and the more you practice, the better you'll be at interpreting it all." (Get started on your own maps by visiting mapmaker.nationalgeographic.org today!)

THE POLITICAL WORLD

Earth's land area is made up of seven continents, but people have divided much of the land into smaller political units called countries. Australia is a continent made up of a single country, and Antarctica is used for scientific research. But the other five continents include almost 200 independent countries. The political map shown here depicts boundaries—imaginary lines created by treaties—that separate countries. Some boundaries, such as the one between the United States and Canada, are very stable and have been recognized for many years.

See Europe map for more detail.

Winkel Tripel Projection

Meridian of Greenwich (London)

Other boundaries, such as the one between Sudan and South Sudan in northeast Africa, are relatively new and still disputed. Countries come in all shapes and sizes. Russia and Canada are giants; others, such as El Salvador and Qatar, are small. Some countries are long and skinny—look at Chile in South America! Still other countries—such as Indonesia and Japan in Asia—are made up of groups of islands. The political map is a clue to the diversity that makes Earth so fascinating.

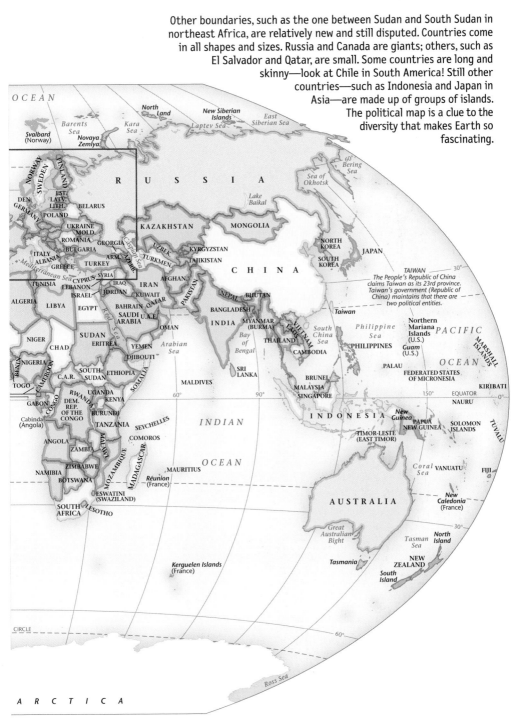

TAIWAN
The People's Republic of China claims Taiwan as its 23rd province. Taiwan's government (Republic of China) maintains that there are two political entities.

THE PHYSICAL WORLD

Earth is dominated by large landmasses called continents—seven in all—and by an interconnected global ocean that is divided into four parts by the continents. More than 70 percent of Earth's surface is covered by oceans, and the rest is made up of land areas.

Different landforms give variety to the surface of the continents. The Rocky Mountains divide North America, the Andes mark the western edge of South America, and the Himalaya tower above South Asia. The Plateau of Tibet forms the rugged core of Asia, while

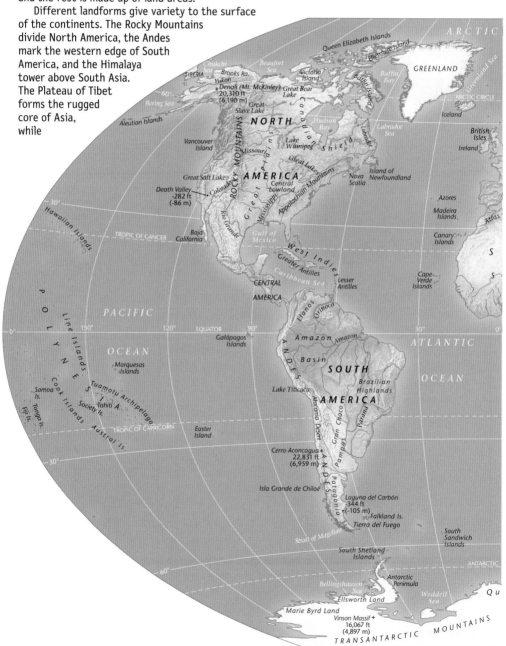

the Northern European Plain extends from the North Sea to the Ural Mountains. Much of Africa is a plateau, and dry plains cover large areas of Australia. Mountains rise more than 16,000 feet (4,877 m) above Antarctica's massive ice sheets. Mountains and trenches make the ocean floors as varied as any continent. A mountain chain called the Mid-Atlantic Ridge runs the length of the Atlantic Ocean. In the western Pacific, trenches drop deep into the ocean floor.

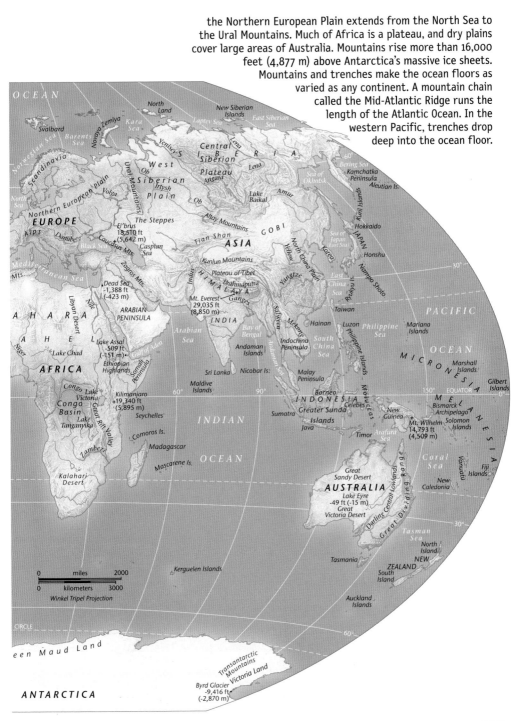

OCEAN

North Land
New Siberian Islands
East Siberian Sea
Laptev Sea
Svalbard
Kara Sea
Novaya Zemlya
Barents Sea
Norwegian Sea
Scandinavia
Yenisey
Central Siberian Plateau
S I B E R I A
Lena
Bering Sea
Kamchatka Peninsula
Aleutian Is.
North Sea
Northern European Plain
Ural Mountains
Volga
West Siberian Plain
Ob
Irtysh
Angara
Lena
Ob
Sea of Okhotsk
Kuril Islands
EUROPE
The Steppes
El'brus 18,510 ft (5,642 m)
Altay Mountains
Lake Baikal
Amur
Hokkaido
Sea of Japan (East Sea)
JAPAN
Alps
Danube
Caucasus Mts.
Black Sea
Caspian Sea
Tian Shan
GOBI
ASIA
Korea
Honshu
Mediterranean Sea
Mts.
Zagros Mts.
Kunlun Mountains
North China Plain
Yellow
Nampo Shoto
Dead Sea -1,388 ft (-423 m)
ARABIAN PENINSULA
Plateau of Tibet
Indus
H I M A L A Y A
Brahmaputra
Ganges
Yangtze
East China Sea
S A H A R A
Libyan Desert
Nile
Mt. Everest 29,035 ft (8,850 m)
INDIA
Arabian Sea
Salween
Mekong
Taiwan
PACIFIC
S A H E L
Lake Assal -509 ft (-151 m)
Gulf of Aden
Bay of Bengal
Hainan
Luzon
Philippine Islands
Mariana Islands
Niger
Lake Chad
Ethiopian Highlands
Somali Peninsula
Andaman Islands
Indochina Peninsula
South China Sea
Philippine Sea
OCEAN
AFRICA
Sri Lanka
Nicobar Is.
Malay Peninsula
M I C R O N E S I A
Marshall Islands
Congo
Lake Victoria
Kilimanjaro +19,340 ft (5,895 m)
Maldive Islands
Borneo
Celebes
Greater Sunda Islands
Moluccas
New Guinea
Gilbert Islands
Congo Basin
Lake Tanganyika
Seychelles
INDIAN
Sumatra
Java
INDONESIA
Bismarck Archipelago
Mt. Wilhelm 14,793 ft (4,509 m)
Solomon Islands
EQUATOR
M E L A N E S I A
Zambezi
Comoros Is.
Madagascar
OCEAN
Timor
Arafura Sea
Coral Sea
Vanuatu
Fiji Islands
Mascarene Is.
Great Sandy Desert
New Caledonia
Kalahari Desert
AUSTRALIA
Lake Eyre -49 ft (-15 m)
Great Victoria Desert
Darling
Central Lowlands
Great Dividing Range
Tasman Sea
New North Island
NEW ZEALAND
Kerguelen Islands
Tasmania
South Island
Auckland Islands

0 miles 2000
0 kilometers 3000
Winkel Tripel Projection

CIRCLE
een Maud Land
Transantarctic Mountains
Byrd Glacier -9,416 ft (-2,870 m)
Victoria Land
ANTARCTICA

KINDS OF MAPS

Maps are special tools that geographers use to tell a story about Earth. Maps can be used to show just about anything related to places. Some maps show physical features, such as mountains or vegetation. Maps can also show climates or natural hazards and other things we cannot easily see. Other maps illustrate different features on Earth—political boundaries, urban centers, and economic systems.

AN IMPERFECT TOOL

Maps are not perfect. A globe is a scale model of Earth with accurate relative sizes and locations. Because maps are flat, they involve distortions of size, shape, and direction. Also, cartographers—people who create maps—make choices about what information to include. Because of this, it is important to study many different types of maps to learn the complete story of Earth. Three commonly found kinds of maps are shown on this page.

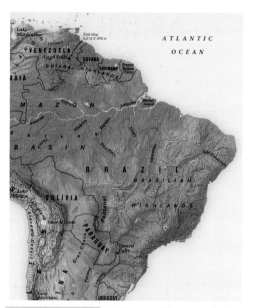

PHYSICAL MAPS. Earth's natural features—landforms, water bodies, and vegetation—are shown on physical maps. The map above uses color and shading to illustrate mountains, lakes, rivers, and deserts of central South America. Country names and borders are added for reference, but they are not natural features.

POLITICAL MAPS. These maps represent characteristics of the landscape created by humans, such as boundaries, cities, and place-names. Natural features are added only for reference. On the map above, capital cities are represented with a star inside a circle, while other cities are shown with black dots.

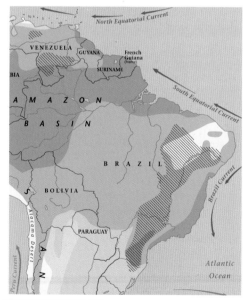

THEMATIC MAPS. Patterns related to a particular topic or theme, such as population distribution, appear on these maps. The map above displays the region's climate zones, which range from tropical wet (bright green) to tropical wet and dry (light green) to semiarid (dark yellow) to arid or desert (light yellow).

MAKING MAPS

Long ago, cartographers worked with pen and ink, carefully handcrafting maps based on explorers' observations and diaries. Today, mapmaking is a high-tech business. Cartographers use Earth data stored in "layers" in a Geographic Information System (GIS) and special computer programs to create maps that can be easily updated as new information becomes available.

National Geographic staff cartographers Mike McNey and Rosemary Wardley review a map of Africa for the *National Geographic Kids World Atlas.*

Satellites in orbit around Earth act as eyes in the sky, recording data about the planet's land and ocean areas. The data is converted to numbers that are transmitted back to computers that are specially programmed to interpret the data. They record it in a form that cartographers can use to create maps.

MAP
PROJECTIONS

To create a map, cartographers transfer an image of the round Earth to a flat surface, a process called projection. All projections involve distortion. For example, an interrupted projection (bottom map) shows accurate shapes and relative sizes of land areas, but oceans have gaps. Other types of projections are cylindrical, conic, or azimuthal—each with certain advantages, but all with some distortion.

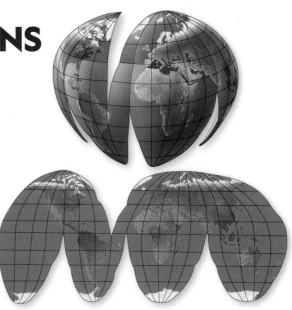

261

GEOGRAPHIC FEATURES

From roaring rivers to parched deserts, from underwater canyons to jagged mountains, Earth is covered with beautiful and diverse environments. Here are examples of the most common types of geographic features found around the world.

WATERFALL

Waterfalls form when a river reaches an abrupt change in elevation. At left, the Iguazú waterfall system—on the border of Brazil and Argentina—is made up of 275 falls.

VALLEY

Valleys, cut by running water or moving ice, may be broad and flat or narrow and steep, such as the Indus River Valley in Ladakh, India (above).

RIVER

As a river moves through flatlands, it twists and turns. Above, the Rio Los Amigos winds through a rain forest in Peru.

MOUNTAIN

Mountains are Earth's tallest landforms, and Mount Everest (above) rises highest of all, at 29,035 feet (8,850 m) above sea level.

GLACIER

Glaciers—"rivers" of ice—such as Alaska's Hubbard Glacier (above) move slowly from mountains to the sea. Global warming is shrinking them.

CANYON

Steep-sided valleys called canyons are created mainly by running water. Buckskin Gulch in Utah (above) is the deepest "slot" canyon in the American Southwest.

DESERT

Deserts are land features created by climate, specifically by a lack of water. Here, a camel caravan crosses the Sahara in North Africa.

7 awesome facts about Earth

1 There are **volcanoes inside glaciers in Iceland.**

2 Antarctica is the only **continent** with **no rain forests.**

3 There are more **geysers** in U.S.A.'s **Yellowstone National Park** than anywhere else on **Earth.**

4 More than **100** million years ago, **India** was an island.

5 The **oldest water on Earth—** some 1 to 2.5 billion years old— **was found 1.5 miles** (2.4 km) down a mine in **Canada.**

6 The **ocean below** the **North Pole** is more than **13,000** feet (3,960 m) **deep.**

7 **Two lakes** continue to **exist** in the **Sahara,** fed by water from **underground.**

Old Faithful geyser, in Yellowstone National Park, Wyoming, U.S.A.

AFRICA

In 1979 and 2012, snow fell in parts of the Sahara in North Africa.

A zebra's night vision is thought to be as good as an owl's.

Zebra

The massive continent of Africa, where humankind began millions of years ago, is second only to Asia in size. Stretching nearly as far from west to east as it does from north to south, Africa is home to both the longest river in the world (the Nile) and the largest hot desert on Earth (the Sahara).

The Great Sphinx at Giza in Egypt

SPEEDY SPECIES

Some of the world's fastest animals live in Africa, such as cheetahs, pronghorn antelopes, wildebeests, and lions. Each of these species can reach speeds topping 50 miles an hour (80 km/h).

ADVANCED ANCESTORS

Our earliest ancestors lived in Africa—and experts say these humans were rather evolved. Artifacts recently discovered in Kenya from some 320,000 years ago show that the *Homo sapiens*—our early ancestor—made tools with sharp blades from volcanic rock and created their own bright red dye from clay, which they may have used as body paint. Scientists think this early civilization also traded for goods with other groups in distant lands, a surprisingly sophisticated system for people who lived so long ago.

Protecting the Environment

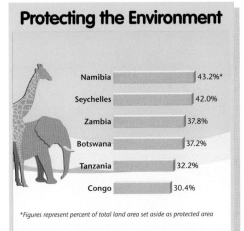

Country	Percent
Namibia	43.2%*
Seychelles	42.0%
Zambia	37.8%
Botswana	37.2%
Tanzania	32.2%
Congo	30.4%

*Figures represent percent of total land area set aside as protected area

MAJOR MINES

Bling it on! Africa is home to many gold and diamond mines, including the deepest mine in the world. The Mponeng mine in South Africa is deeper than 13,000 feet (3,960 m) and features tunnels that are many miles long. It takes over an hour to get to the bottom, where temps top 140°F (60°C). As for diamonds? Botswana's Jwaneng mine produces up to 15 million carats of bling every year—making it the world's most valuable diamond mine.

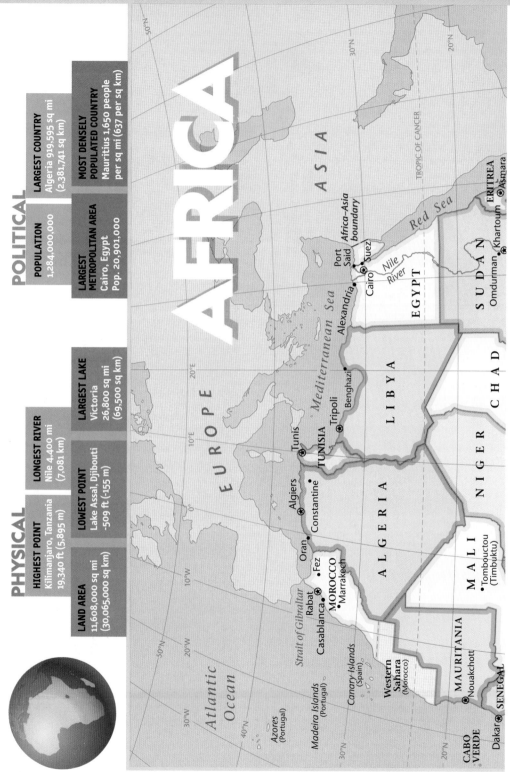

AFRICA

PHYSICAL

LAND AREA
11,608,000 sq mi
(30,065,000 sq km)

HIGHEST POINT
Kilimanjaro, Tanzania
19,340 ft (5,895 m)

LOWEST POINT
Lake Assal, Djibouti
-509 ft (-155 m)

LONGEST RIVER
Nile 4,400 mi
(7,081 km)

LARGEST LAKE
Victoria
26,800 sq mi
(69,500 sq km)

POLITICAL

POPULATION
1,284,000,000

**LARGEST
METROPOLITAN AREA**
Cairo, Egypt
Pop. 20,901,000

LARGEST COUNTRY
Algeria 919,595 sq mi
(2,381,741 sq km)

**MOST DENSELY
POPULATED COUNTRY**
Mauritius 1,650 people
per sq mi (637 per sq km)

EUROPE

ASIA

Atlantic
Ocean

Mediterranean Sea

Red Sea

TROPIC OF CANCER

Azores
(Portugal)

Madeira Islands
(Portugal)

Canary Islands
(Spain)

Strait of Gibraltar

Rabat
Casablanca
MOROCCO
Marrakech
Fez
Oran
Constantine
Algiers
Tunis
TUNISIA
Tripoli
Benghazi

ALGERIA

LIBYA

EGYPT

Alexandria
Port
Said
Cairo
Suez
Africa-Asia
boundary
Nile
River

Western
Sahara
(Morocco)

MAURITANIA
Nouakchott

MALI
Tombouctou
(Timbuktu)

NIGER

CHAD

SUDAN

Omdurman
Khartoum

ERITREA
Asmara

CABO
VERDE

Dakar
SENEGAL

50°N
40°N
30°N
20°N

30°W
20°W
10°W
0°
10°E
20°E
30°E

50°N
30°N
20°N

266

Map Key

⊛ National capital
• Other city
▲ Highest point
▾ Lowest point

800 Miles
800 Kilometers

Azimuthal Equal-Area Projection

ANTARCTICA

Gentoo penguin

There are mountains buried under ice in Antarctica.

An adult gentoo penguin makes as many as 450 dives a day looking for food.

This frozen continent may be a cool place to visit, but unless you're a penguin, you probably wouldn't want to hang out in Antarctica for long. The fact that it's the coldest, windiest, and driest continent helps explain why humans never colonized this ice-covered land surrounding the South Pole.

Weddell seal

GOING THE DISTANCE

Each year, a few hundred runners from around the world compete in the Antarctica Marathon and Half-Marathon, a hilly and twisty race along the continent's icy peninsula.

A DAY TO CELEBRATE

DECEMBER 1

Signed in 1959, the Antarctic Treaty, which governs Antarctica, says that the continent should be used only for peaceful purposes. The treaty, which has now been signed by 53 countries, also established Antarctica as a scientific reserve and a place for scientific exploration. Any activities that may disrupt the natural environment are prohibited. Each year on December 1, World Antarctica Day marks the signing of the treaty and celebrates this unique and fascinating place on Earth.

FREAKY FALLS

Five-story-tall Blood Falls in Antarctica oozes red water from an ancient lake trapped under Taylor Glacier. First discovered in 1911, the falls' creepy color baffled experts, who originally thought it came from red algae. But recent studies show that the lake deep beneath the glacier is super-salty and full of iron, which turns the water red. Another fascinating fact about the falls? Scientists say it takes approximately 1.5 million years for the ancient lake water to travel through tiny cracks and channels in Taylor Glacier before it sees the light of day.

Earth's Largest Deserts

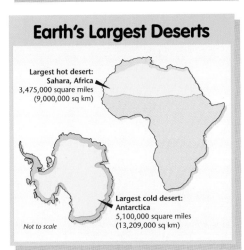

Largest hot desert: Sahara, Africa 3,475,000 square miles (9,000,000 sq km)

Largest cold desert: Antarctica 5,100,000 square miles (13,209,000 sq km)

Not to scale

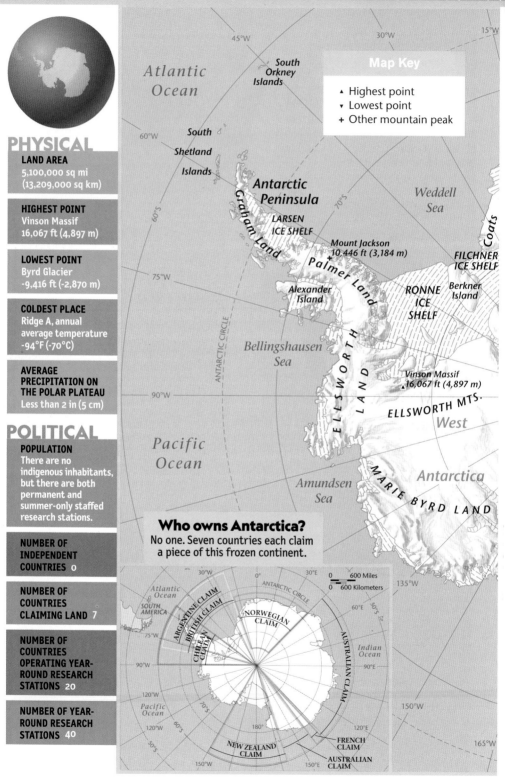

PHYSICAL

LAND AREA
5,100,000 sq mi
(13,209,000 sq km)

HIGHEST POINT
Vinson Massif
16,067 ft (4,897 m)

LOWEST POINT
Byrd Glacier
-9,416 ft (-2,870 m)

COLDEST PLACE
Ridge A, annual
average temperature
-94°F (-70°C)

**AVERAGE
PRECIPITATION ON
THE POLAR PLATEAU**
Less than 2 in (5 cm)

POLITICAL

POPULATION
There are no
indigenous inhabitants,
but there are both
permanent and
summer-only staffed
research stations.

**NUMBER OF
INDEPENDENT
COUNTRIES** 0

**NUMBER OF
COUNTRIES
CLAIMING LAND** 7

**NUMBER OF
COUNTRIES
OPERATING YEAR-
ROUND RESEARCH
STATIONS** 20

**NUMBER OF YEAR-
ROUND RESEARCH
STATIONS** 40

Map Key
▲ Highest point
▼ Lowest point
+ Other mountain peak

Atlantic Ocean

South Orkney Islands

South Shetland Islands

Antarctic Peninsula

Graham Land

LARSEN ICE SHELF

Weddell Sea

Coats

Mount Jackson
10,446 ft (3,184 m)

FILCHNER ICE SHELF

Palmer Land

Alexander Island

RONNE ICE SHELF

Berkner Island

ANTARCTIC CIRCLE

Bellingshausen Sea

ELLSWORTH LAND

Vinson Massif
▲16,067 ft (4,897 m)

ELLSWORTH MTS.

West

Pacific Ocean

Amundsen Sea

MARIE BYRD LAND

Antarctica

Who owns Antarctica?
No one. Seven countries each claim
a piece of this frozen continent.

Atlantic Ocean

SOUTH AMERICA

ANTARCTIC CIRCLE

ARGENTINE CLAIM

BRITISH CLAIM

CHILEAN CLAIM

NORWEGIAN CLAIM

Indian Ocean

AUSTRALIAN CLAIM

Pacific Ocean

NEW ZEALAND CLAIM

FRENCH CLAIM

AUSTRALIAN CLAIM

0   600 Miles
0   600 Kilometers

270

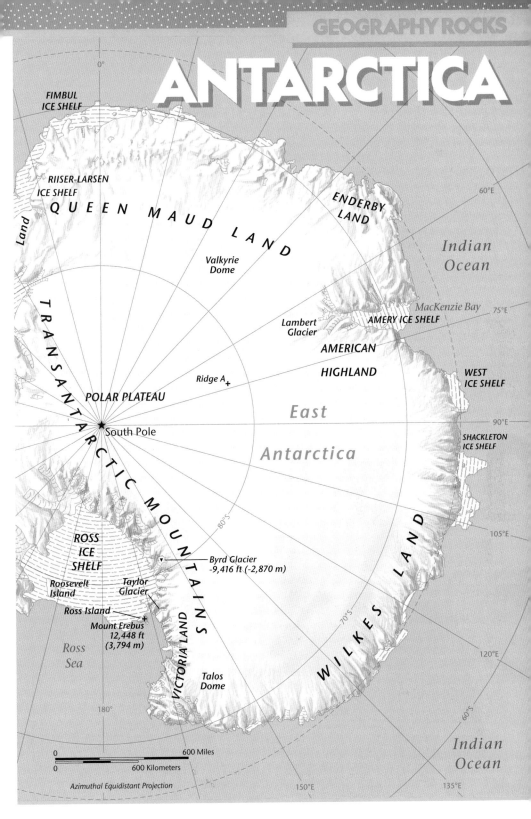

ANTARCTICA

FIMBUL
ICE SHELF

0°

RIISER-LARSEN
ICE SHELF

ENDERBY
LAND

60°E

Q U E E N   M A U D   L A N D

Land

Indian
Ocean

Valkyrie
Dome

Lambert
Glacier

MacKenzie Bay

75°E

AMERY ICE SHELF

AMERICAN

T R A N S A N T A R C T I C

Ridge A +

HIGHLAND

WEST
ICE SHELF

POLAR PLATEAU

East

90°E

South Pole

Antarctica

SHACKLETON
ICE SHELF

105°E

M O U N T A I N S

80°S

ROSS
ICE
SHELF

Byrd Glacier
-9,416 ft (-2,870 m)

Roosevelt
Island

Taylor
Glacier

W I L K E S   L A N D

Ross Island

70°S

120°E

Mount Erebus
12,448 ft
(3,794 m)

VICTORIA LAND

Ross
Sea

Talos
Dome

60°S

180°

Indian
Ocean

0   600 Miles

0   600 Kilometers

Azimuthal Equidistant Projection

150°E

135°E

271

ASIA

Children with a water buffalo in Sa Pa, Vietnam

A water buffalo's wide hooves keep it from sinking in mud.

About 73 percent of Japan is covered with mountains.

Made up of 46 countries, Asia is the world's largest continent. Just how big is it? From western Turkey to the eastern tip of Russia, Asia spans nearly half the globe! Home to more than four billion citizens—that's three out of five people on the planet—Asia's population is bigger than that of all the other continents combined.

Kuala Lumpur, Malaysia

ON THE MOVE

About a third of the population of Mongolia moves seasonally. They live in portable huts called *ger* while traveling up to 70 miles (112 km) on foot to find food sources for their livestock.

ON THE BORDER

Asia is the only continent that shares borders with two other continents: Africa and Europe. Here a marker identifies the border between Europe and Asia in western Russia.

GOING BATTY

From the hefty golden-crowned flying fox to the itty-bitty bumblebee bat, Asia is home to at least 435 of the world's more than 1,300 species of bats. Indonesia has the world's largest number of species, with more than 175 different types of bats. And in Malaysia? Bats outnumber all other mammals in the country, including humans! The winged mammals help keep the ecosystem healthy, especially in Southeast Asia's forests where the bats play a key role in spreading the seeds of trees and other plants.

Tallest Peaks by Continent

Everest, *Asia*
Aconcagua, *South America*
Denali, *North America*
Kilimanjaro, *Africa*
El'brus, *Europe*
Vinson Massif, *Antarctica*

Kosciusko, *Australia**

sea level   *Does not include Oceania*

PHYSICAL

LAND AREA
17,208,000 sq mi
(44,570,000 sq km)

HIGHEST POINT
Mount Everest,
China–Nepal
29,035 ft (8,850 m)

LOWEST POINT
Dead Sea,
Israel–Jordan
-1,388 ft (-423 m)

LONGEST RIVER
Yangtze, China
3,880 mi (6,244 km)

**LARGEST LAKE
ENTIRELY IN ASIA**
Lake Baikal, Russia
12,200 sq mi
(31,500 sq km)

POLITICAL

POPULATION
4,536,000,000

**LARGEST
METROPOLITAN AREA**
Tokyo, Japan
Pop. 37,393,000

**LARGEST COUNTRY
ENTIRELY IN ASIA**
China
3,705,406 sq mi
(9,596,960 sq km)

**MOST DENSELY
POPULATED COUNTRY**
Singapore
22,745 people
per sq mi
(8,788 per sq km)

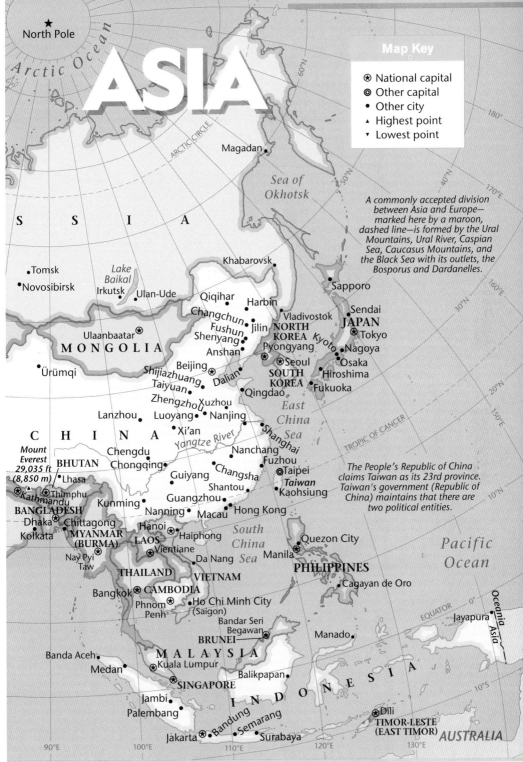

★ North Pole

Arctic Ocean

R U S S I A

ASIA

Map Key

⊛ National capital
◉ Other capital
• Other city
▲ Highest point
▼ Lowest point

A commonly accepted division between Asia and Europe—marked here by a maroon, dashed line—is formed by the Ural Mountains, Ural River, Caspian Sea, Caucasus Mountains, and the Black Sea with its outlets, the Bosporus and Dardanelles.

Magadan

Sea of Okhotsk

ARCTIC CIRCLE

•Tomsk
•Novosibirsk
Lake Baikal
Irkutsk •Ulan-Ude
Khabarovsk
Sapporo

Qiqihar Harbin
Changchun •Jilin •Vladivostok
Fushun
Shenyang NORTH KOREA
Anshan Pyongyang
Sendai
JAPAN
⊛Tokyo
Kyoto
Nagoya

Ulaanbaatar⊛
M O N G O L I A

•Ürümqi
Beijing⊛
Shijiazhuang• •Dalian
Taiyuan•
Zhengzhou•Xuzhou
Lanzhou• Luoyang• •Nanjing

⊛Seoul
SOUTH KOREA
Hiroshima
Osaka
Fukuoka
Qingdao

East China Sea

TROPIC OF CANCER

C H I N A •Xi'an
Yangtze River
Shanghai

Mount Everest 29,035 ft (8,850 m)
BHUTAN
Chengdu
Chongqing•
Guiyang•
•Changsha
Nanchang•
Fuzhou
Taipei
Taiwan
Kaohsiung

The People's Republic of China claims Taiwan as its 23rd province. Taiwan's government (Republic of China) maintains that there are two political entities.

▲Kathmandu
BANGLADESH
Dhaka⊛
Kolkata•
MYANMAR (BURMA)
Thimphu
Lhasa
Kunming•
Shantou•
Guangzhou•
Nanning• •Macau Hong Kong

Chittagong
Hanoi⊛
Nay Pyi Taw
LAOS
•Haiphong
•Vientiane
South China Sea

Quezon City

Pacific Ocean

THAILAND
Bangkok⊛
VIETNAM
CAMBODIA
Phnom⊛
Penh
Da Nang Manila
PHILIPPINES
Cagayan de Oro

Ho Chi Minh City (Saigon)
Bandar Seri Begawan⊛
BRUNEI
Manado•

EQUATOR
Jayapura

Oceania
Asia

Banda Aceh•
Medan•
M A L A Y S I A
•Kuala Lumpur
Balikpapan•
⊛SINGAPORE
I N D O N E S I A

Jambi•
Palembang•
Bandung
Semarang
Jakarta⊛
Surabaya

Dili
TIMOR-LESTE (EAST TIMOR)
AUSTRALIA

90°E   100°E   110°E   120°E   130°E

AUSTRALIA,
NEW ZEALAND, AND OCEANIA

More than one-third of New Zealand's population lives in the city of Auckland.

Australia's capitol building was designed in the shape of a boomerang.

Auckland Harbour in Auckland, New Zealand

G'day, mate! This vast region, covering almost 3.3 million square miles (8.5 million sq km), includes Australia—the world's smallest and flattest continent—and New Zealand, as well as a fleet of mostly tiny islands scattered across the Pacific Ocean. Also known as "down under," most of the countries in this region are in the Southern Hemisphere, and below the Equator.

Aboriginal children of Australia in ceremonial dress

ROCK STARS

Most of Australia is a rural desert, also known as the outback. Here you can also find a giant rock formation called Uluru, or Ayers Rock, which appears to change color during the day.

FOR THE DOGS

Dingos are wild dogs found almost exclusively in Australia. But these canines aren't actually native to down under—they likely arrived 1,000–5,000 years ago by boat from Asia. Today, these social dogs travel in packs throughout the forests, plains, mountains, and deserts of northern, northwestern, and central Australia. As the largest land predator in Australia, they prey on small to medium animals, such as lizards, rodents, and rabbits.

Sizing Up the Great Barrier Reef

Just how big is the Great Barrier Reef Marine Park? It's approximately as large as:

Great Barrier Reef Marine Park

Germany

Vietnam

Australia

or the Republic of Congo

*Based on an area of 133,000 square miles (344,400 sq km)

GROW ON

About 80 percent of the plants in New Zealand are not found anywhere else in the world. And some of them doubled as dinosaur snacks! Plants like the kauri—a coniferous tree—have ancestors that date back to the Jurassic period. And New Zealand's magnificent lowland forests have been nicknamed "dinosaur forests" because of the prehistoric plants that grow there.

PHYSICAL

LAND AREA
3,278,000 sq mi
(8,490,000 sq km)

HIGHEST POINT*
Mount Wilhelm,
Papua New Guinea
14,793 ft (4,509 m)
*includes Oceania

LOWEST POINT
Lake Eyre, Australia
-49 ft (-15 m)

LONGEST RIVER
Murray-Darling,
Australia
2,282 mi (3,672 km)

LARGEST LAKE
Lake Eyre, Australia
3,741 sq mi
(9,690 sq km)

POLITICAL

POPULATION
41,000,000

**LARGEST
METROPOLITAN AREA**
Melbourne, Australia
Pop. 4,968,000

LARGEST COUNTRY
Australia
2,988,901 sq mi
(7,741,220 sq km)

**MOST DENSELY
POPULATED COUNTRY**
Nauru
1,250 people per sq mi
(476 per sq km)

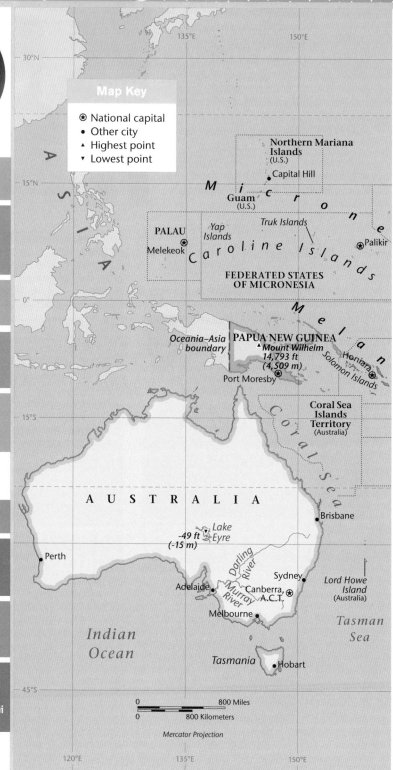

Map Key

⊛ National capital
• Other city
▲ Highest point
▾ Lowest point

Northern Mariana
Islands
(U.S.)
• Capital Hill

Guam
(U.S.)

M i c r o n e

Yap   Truk Islands
PALAU   Islands
Melekeok ⊛   ⊛ Palikir
C a r o l i n e   I s l a n d s

FEDERATED STATES
OF MICRONESIA

M e l a

PAPUA NEW GUINEA
Oceania–Asia   ▲ Mount Wilhelm
boundary   14,793 ft
                 (4,509 m)   Honiara ⊛
                                   Solomon Islands
Port Moresby

Coral Sea
Islands
Territory
(Australia)

A U S T R A L I A   • Brisbane

                 ▾Lake
         -49 ft Eyre
         (-15 m)

• Perth   Darling
                                     River   Sydney •   Lord Howe
                 Adelaide • Murray   Island
                           River Canberra,   (Australia)
                                  A.C.T. ⊛
                 Melbourne •

**Indian
Ocean**
                                              Tasman
                 Tasmania • Hobart   Sea

0   800 Miles
0   800 Kilometers

Mercator Projection

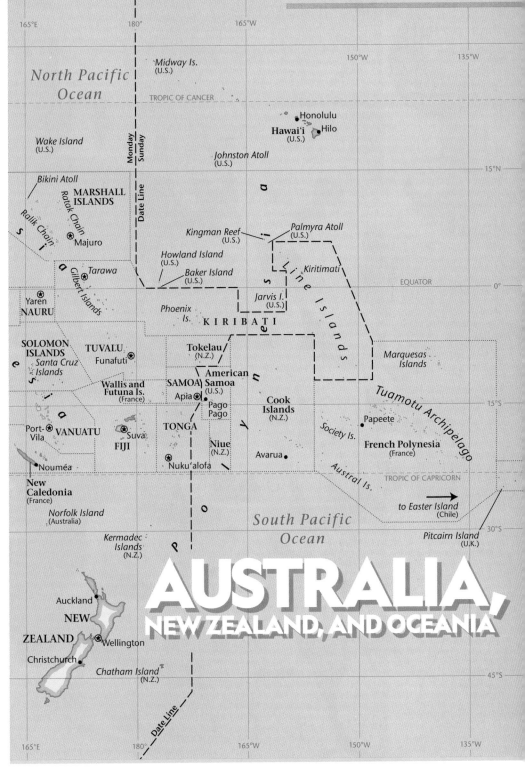

165°E · 180° · 165°W · 150°W · 135°W

North Pacific Ocean

Midway Is. (U.S.)

TROPIC OF CANCER

Honolulu
Hawai'i Hilo
(U.S.)

Wake Island (U.S.)

Monday | Sunday

Date Line

Johnston Atoll (U.S.)

15°N

Bikini Atoll

MARSHALL ISLANDS

Ralik Chain · Rattak Chain

Majuro

Kingman Reef (N.Z.)

Palmyra Atoll (U.S.)

Howland Island (U.S.)

Tarawa

Gilbert Islands

Baker Island (U.S.)

Kiritimati

EQUATOR · 0°

Yaren
NAURU

Jarvis I. (U.S.)

Line Islands

Phoenix Is. **K I R I B A T I**

SOLOMON ISLANDS
Santa Cruz Islands

TUVALU
Funafuti

Tokelau (N.Z.)

Marquesas Islands

Tuamotu Archipelago

15°S

Wallis and Futuna Is. (France)

SAMOA **American Samoa** (U.S.)
Apia
Pago Pago

Cook Islands (N.Z.)

Society Is.

Papeete

Port-Vila **VANUATU**

Suva
FIJI

TONGA

Niue (N.Z.)

Avarua

French Polynesia (France)

Nuku'alofa

Austral Is.

TROPIC OF CAPRICORN

Nouméa

New Caledonia (France)

Norfolk Island (Australia)

to Easter Island (Chile)

30°S

Kermadec Islands (N.Z.)

South Pacific Ocean

Pitcairn Island (U.K.)

AUSTRALIA,
NEW ZEALAND, AND OCEANIA

Auckland

NEW ZEALAND

Wellington

Christchurch

Chatham Island (N.Z.)

45°S

Date Line

165°E · 180° · 165°W · 150°W · 135°W

EUROPE

A pastry chef in Paris is known for his foie gras macarons—or goose liver cookies.

It's considered rude to write in red ink in Portugal.

Macarons in a pastry shop

A cluster of islands and peninsulas jutting west from Asia, Europe is bordered by the Atlantic and Arctic Oceans and more than a dozen seas. Here you'll find a variety of scenery, from mountains to countryside to coastlines. Europe is also known for its rich culture and fascinating history, which make it one of the most visited continents on Earth.

Traditional dance performed in Greece

SPOT IT

Dalmatians get their name from Dalmatia, a region of Croatia along the Adriatic Sea. The spotted canines have served as border guard dogs during conflicts in the region.

BERRY GOOD

Most of the world's raspberries are grown in Europe. Russia, Serbia, and Poland rank among the world's leading producers. The fertile soil and temperate climate in those countries create ideal growing conditions. Raspberries are native to Europe, and there are records of them being cultivated in Greece and Turkey more than 2,000 years ago. Now that's some sweet history!

SEEING THE LIGHT

The midnight sun is a natural phenomenon that occurs every summer near the Arctic Circle when the sun can still be seen at midnight. Several places in northern Europe—including parts of Iceland, Norway, Finland, Sweden, Denmark, and Russia—experience the phenomena. Svalbard, Norway, experiences the longest period of the midnight sun in that country, with the sun staying visible in the night sky between April 20 and August 22.

Europe's Longest Rivers

Volga	2,290 miles (3,685 km)
Danube	1,770 miles (2,848 km)
Dnieper	1,420 miles (2,285 km)
Rhine	765 miles (1,230 km)
Elbe	724 miles (1,165 km)

PHYSICAL

LAND AREA
3,841,000 sq mi
(9,947,000 sq km)

HIGHEST POINT
El'brus, Russia
18,510 ft (5,642 m)

LOWEST POINT
Caspian Sea
-92 ft (-28 m)

LONGEST RIVER
Volga, Russia
2,290 mi
(3,685 km)

**LARGEST LAKE
ENTIRELY IN EUROPE**
Ladoga, Russia
6,900 sq mi
(17,872 sq km)

POLITICAL

POPULATION
746,000,000

**LARGEST
METROPOLITAN AREA**
Moscow, Russia
Pop. 12,538,000

**LARGEST COUNTRY
ENTIRELY IN EUROPE**
Ukraine
233,030 sq mi
(603,550 sq km)

**MOST DENSELY
POPULATED COUNTRY**
Monaco
50,000 people per sq
mi (20,000 per sq km)

Map Key

⊛ National capital
• Other city
▫ Small country
▲ Highest point
▼ Lowest point

30°W · 20°W · 10°W · 0°

Jan Mayen
(Norway)

Reykjavík
ICELAND

60°N

ARCTIC CIRCLE

Norwegian
Sea

Faroe Islands
(Denmark)

PRIME MERIDIAN

Shetland
Islands

Orkney Islands

Oslo

SCOTLAND
Glasgow · Edinburgh
N. IRELAND · Belfast
IRELAND
(ÉIRE) · Dublin · UNITED KINGDOM
Liverpool · Manchester
WALES · Birmingham
Cardiff · ENGLAND
London ⊛ · The Hague · NETH. · Hamburg
Amsterdam · Berlin ⊛

North
Sea

Göteborg

DENMARK
Copenhagen ⊛
Kiel

50°N

Atlantic
Ocean

Brussels ⊛
BELGIUM
⊛ Paris
Nantes

GERMANY
Frankfurt
LUX. · Prague
Munich
LIECH.

Bay of
Biscay

FRANCE · Zürich
Bern · SWITZ. · AUSTRIA
Bordeaux · Lyon · Milan · Ljubljana
Turin · Venice · SLOV.
Genoa

40°N

Oporto
PORTUGAL
Bilbao
Valladolid
Lisbon · Madrid ⊛
ANDORRA
Zaragoza
10°W
SPAIN
Valencia
Seville · Murcia
Málaga
Gibraltar (U.K.)

Toulouse
MONACO
Nice
Marseille
Corsica
(France)
Barcelona
Balearic Is.
(Spain)

SAN ▫
MARINO
ITALY
VATICAN
CITY ⊛
Rome
Naples

Sardinia
(Italy)

Mediterra

Messina
Palermo
Catania
Sicily

AFRICA

Valletta ⊛
MALTA

0 · 400 Miles
0 · 400 Kilometers
Azimuthal Equidistant Projection

10°E

282

Barents Sea

10°E 20°E 30°E 40°E 50°E 60°E 70°E

•Murmansk

60°N

Asia
Europe

ASIA

N O R W A Y

S W E D E N

•Archangel

RUSSIA

FINLAND

EUROPE

Lake
Ladoga

⊛Helsinki

Tallinn ⊛
⊛Stockholm

St. Petersburg

Yaroslavl' Kazan'   •Ufa

Tver'   Volga River

Nizhniy
⊛Moscow Novgorod

Samara Orenburg

50°N

ESTONIA

Baltic Sea

Riga ⊛

LATVIA

Ryazan'•

LITHUANIA Vitsyebsk•
Kaliningrad
(Russia) ⊛Vilnius •Smolensk •Penza

Gdańsk• Kaunas

⊛Minsk •Bryansk Saratov•

POLAND BELARUS

Bydgoszcz• ⊛Warsaw Homyel'• •Kursk KAZAKHSTAN

•Łódź

•Wrocław •Kraków ⊛Kiev •Kharkiv Volgograd•

CZECHIA
(CZECH REP.) Poltava•

•L'viv U K R A I N E Donets'k Astrakhan'•

Vinnytsya •Rostov

Vienna •Dnipropetrovs'k Caspian Sea

SLOVAKIA MOLDOVA

⊛ ⊛Bratislava ⊛Chişinău -92 ft ▽
(-28 m)

⊛Budapest

HUNGARY ROMANIA •Odesa El'brus Groznyy•

⊛Zagreb CRIMEA (5,642 m) 18,510 ft▲

CROATIA Simferopol'• Sochi GEORGIA Baku⊛

BOSNIA & •Belgrade Bucharest Sevastopol'• AZERBAIJAN
HERZEGOVINA ⊛ 40°N

•Sarajevo SERBIA Black Sea

MONTENEGRO KOSOVO •Varna

•Podgorica ⊛Pristina ⊛BULGARIA

Tirana• ⊛Skopje Sofia

ALBANIA MACED. Istanbul

•Thessaloníki

Dardanelles T U R K E Y

GREECE

A commonly accepted division
between Asia and Europe—
marked here by a maroon,
dashed line—is formed by the
Ural Mountains, Ural River, Caspian
Sea, Caucasus Mountains, and
the Black Sea with its outlets, the
Bosporus and Dardanelles.

⊛Athens

Sea

Crete NORTHERN CYPRUS
Nicosia ⊛

CYPRUS

20°E 30°E 40°E

283

NORTH AMERICA

There are more than 100,000 coffee farms in Mexico.

Polar bears have no natural predators.

Polar bear with cub, Manitoba, Canada

284

From the Great Plains of the United States and Canada to the rain forests of Panama, North America stretches 5,500 miles (8,850 km) from north to south. The third largest continent, North America can be divided into five regions: the mountainous west (including parts of Mexico and Central America's western coast), the Great Plains, the Canadian Shield, the varied eastern region (including Central America's lowlands and coastal plains), and the Caribbean.

Onlookers celebrate the opening of the Panama Canal expansion in 2016.

VIKINGS LIVED HERE

Some 1,000 years ago, a troop of Norse explorers traveled by boat from Norway to the banks of Newfoundland, Canada. There, they found plenty of salmon, wild grapes, and timber—and set up camp. Today, the only known Viking settlement in North America can be found at L'Anse aux Meadows in the northernmost tip of Newfoundland. Archaeological evidence shows that these adventurous seafarers may have spent time in northeastern New Brunswick as well.

HIGH ENERGY

The United States is one of the top producers of geothermal energy—energy from the natural heat of the ground. Among the states, California leads the geothermal charge, with some 5 percent of the state's total power generated from underground heat. In New York City, St. Patrick's Cathedral (above) recently installed a geothermal plant for heating and cooling that stretches as deep as 2,200 feet (670 m) below the building.

TAKING FLIGHT

Millions of monarchs migrate up to 3,000 miles (4,828 km) to Mexico every year from the United States and Canada. They're the only butterflies to make such a massive journey.

World's Longest Coastlines

Canada	151,023 miles (243,048 km)
Indonesia	33,998 miles (54,716 km)
Russia	23,397 miles (37,653 km)
Philippines	22,549 miles (36,289 km)
Japan	18,486 miles (29,751 km)

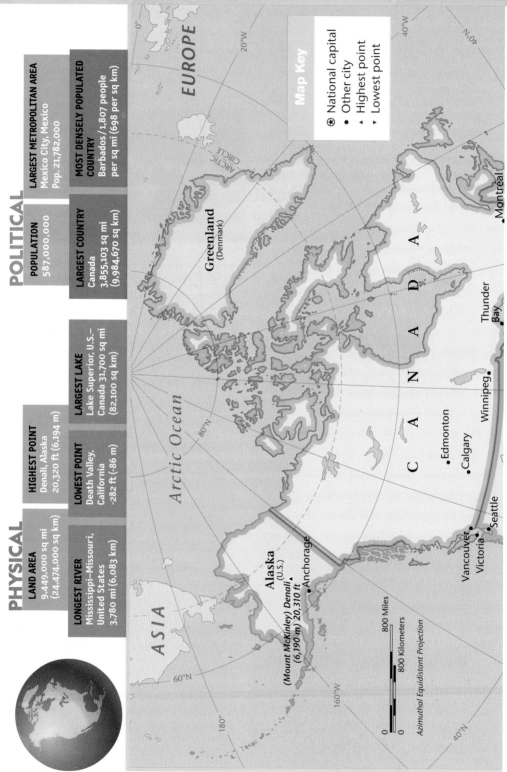

PHYSICAL

LAND AREA
9,449,000 sq mi
(24,474,000 sq km)

LONGEST RIVER
Mississippi–Missouri,
United States
3,780 mi (6,083 km)

HIGHEST POINT
Denali, Alaska
20,320 ft (6,194 m)

LOWEST POINT
Death Valley,
California
-282 ft (-86 m)

LARGEST LAKE
Lake Superior, U.S.–
Canada 31,700 sq mi
(82,100 sq km)

POLITICAL

POPULATION
587,000,000

LARGEST COUNTRY
Canada
3,855,103 sq mi
(9,984,670 sq km)

LARGEST METROPOLITAN AREA
Mexico City, Mexico
Pop. 21,782,000

**MOST DENSELY POPULATED
COUNTRY**
Barbados / 1,807 people
per sq mi (698 per sq km)

Map Key

⊛ National capital
• Other city
▲ Highest point
▼ Lowest point

EUROPE

ARCTIC CIRCLE

Greenland
(Denmark)

Arctic Ocean

ASIA

C A N A D A

Alaska
(U.S.)

(Mount McKinley) Denali ▲
(6,190 m) 20,310 ft

•Anchorage

Edmonton•
Calgary•

Winnipeg•

Thunder
Bay•

Montréal•

Vancouver•
Victoria• •Seattle

0   800 Miles
0   800 Kilometers

Azimuthal Equidistant Projection

180°

160°W

60°N

80°N

0°

20°W

40°W

40°N

40°N

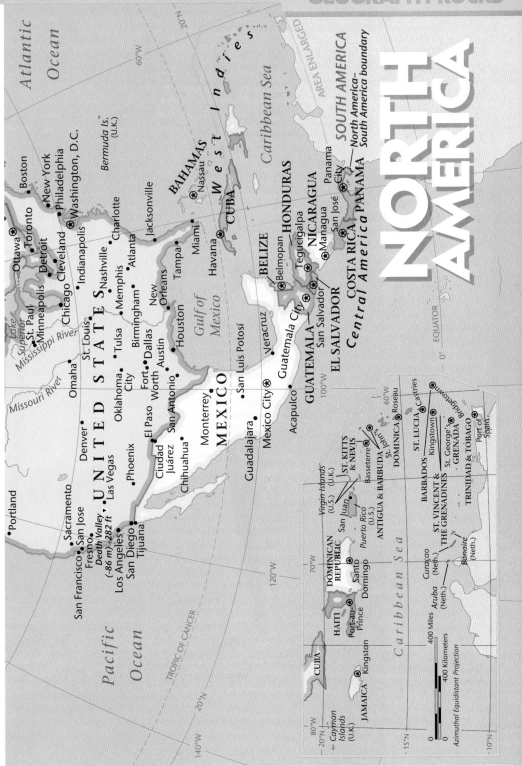

Atlantic Ocean

Pacific Ocean

Caribbean Sea

Gulf of Mexico

West Indies

UNITED STATES

MEXICO

CUBA

BAHAMAS

BELIZE
GUATEMALA
EL SALVADOR
HONDURAS
NICARAGUA
COSTA RICA
PANAMA

Central America

NORTH AMERICA

SOUTH AMERICA
North America–
South America boundary
AREA ENLARGED

Portland
San Francisco
Sacramento
San Jose
Fresno
Death Valley
(–86 m) –282 ft
Los Angeles
San Diego
Tijuana
Las Vegas
Denver
Phoenix
El Paso
Ciudad Juárez
Chihuahua
Oklahoma City
Omaha
Tulsa
Fort Worth
Dallas
San Antonio
Austin
Houston
Monterrey
Guadalajara
San Luis Potosí
Mexico City
Acapulco
Veracruz
Guatemala City
San Salvador
Belmopan
Tegucigalpa
Managua
San José
San Juan
Panama City
Havana
Tampa
Miami
Nassau
Jacksonville
Charlotte
Atlanta
Nashville
Memphis
Birmingham
New Orleans
St. Louis
Indianapolis
Chicago
St. Paul
Minneapolis
Detroit
Cleveland
Ottawa
Toronto
Boston
New York
Philadelphia
Washington, D.C.

Lake Superior
Mississippi River
Missouri River

Bermuda Is.
(U.K.)

TROPIC OF CANCER
EQUATOR

140°W
120°W
100°W
80°W
70°W
60°W
0°
20°N

Azimuthal Equidistant Projection

400 Miles
0
400 Kilometers

Virgin Islands
(U.S.)
Puerto Rico
(U.S.)
CUBA
JAMAICA Kingston
Cayman Islands
(U.K.)
HAITI
Port-au-Prince
DOMINICAN REPUBLIC
Santo Domingo
ST. KITTS & NEVIS
Basseterre
ANTIGUA & BARBUDA
St. John's
DOMINICA Roseau
ST. LUCIA Castries
ST. VINCENT & THE GRENADINES
Kingstown
BARBADOS
Bridgetown
GRENADA
St. George's
TRINIDAD & TOBAGO
Port of Spain
Curaçao
(Neth.)
Aruba
(Neth.)
Bonaire
(Neth.)

Caribbean Sea

15°N
10°N
20°N

SOUTH AMERICA

Brazil has participated in the FIFA World Cup 21 times—more than any other team.

Ancient tombs in Peru contain kernels of popcorn, some of which still pop.

A boy plays soccer in Manaus, Brazil.

South America is bordered by three major bodies of water—the Caribbean Sea, Atlantic Ocean, and Pacific Ocean. The world's fourth largest continent extends over a range of climates from tropical in the north to subarctic in the south. South America produces a rich diversity of natural resources, including nuts, fruits, sugar, grains, coffee, and chocolate.

Santiago Cathedral in Santiago, Chile

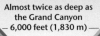

BIG BIRD

The Andean condor, which lives exclusively in the mountains and valleys of the Andes, is the largest raptor in the world and the largest flying bird in South America.

OCEANS ALL AROUND

South America is surrounded by both the Pacific and Atlantic Oceans. Experts think that the two oceans used to be one massive body of water until North and South America joined together at the Isthmus of Panama some three million years ago. That move, scientists think, divided the original ocean into two. Today, Colombia and Chile are the only two countries in South America with a coastline on each ocean.

South America's Deepest Canyon

Peru's Cotahuasi Canyon is more than 11,500 feet (3,500 m) deep!

Almost twice as deep as the Grand Canyon
6,000 feet (1,830 m)

Burj Khalifa
2,717 feet
(828 m)

ICE LAND

Patagonia in southern Chile is home to one of the largest ice fields in the world. The Southern Patagonia Icefield, which stretches across the Andes Mountains and occupies parts of Argentina and Chile, feeds some 50 major glaciers that flow into the Pacific Ocean or freshwater lakes. The ice field takes up an area almost as large as the Bahamas and is so big, it can be seen from space on a clear day.

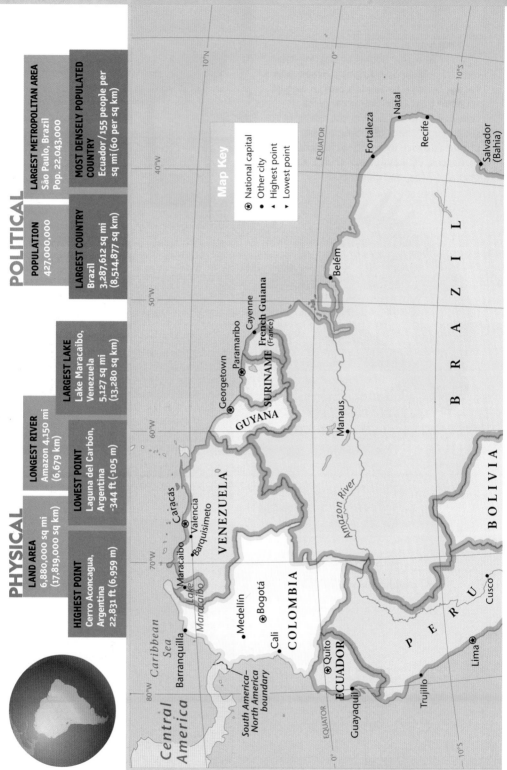

PHYSICAL

HIGHEST POINT	LAND AREA
Cerro Aconcagua, Argentina 22,831 ft (6,959 m)	6,880,000 sq mi (17,819,000 sq km)

LOWEST POINT	LONGEST RIVER
Laguna del Carbón, Argentina -344 ft (-105 m)	Amazon 4,150 mi (6,679 km)

LARGEST LAKE
Lake Maracaibo, Venezuela
5,127 sq mi
(13,280 sq km)

POLITICAL

LARGEST COUNTRY	POPULATION
Brazil 3,287,612 sq mi (8,514,877 sq km)	427,000,000

MOST DENSELY POPULATED COUNTRY	LARGEST METROPOLITAN AREA
Ecuador / 155 people per sq mi (60 per sq km)	São Paulo, Brazil Pop. 22,043,000

Map Key

⊛ National capital
• Other city
▲ Highest point
▼ Lowest point

Central
America

Caribbean
Sea

South America–
North America
boundary

Barranquilla
Maracaibo
Lake
Maracaibo
Medellín
•Bogotá
Cali
COLOMBIA
Valencia
Caracas⊛
Barquisimeto
VENEZUELA

Quito⊛
ECUADOR
Guayaquil
Trujillo
Lima⊛
P E R U
Cusco°

BOLIVIA

Georgetown⊛
GUYANA
Paramaribo⊛
SURINAME
Cayenne
French Guiana
(France)

Manaus

Amazon River

B R A Z I L

Belém
Fortaleza
Natal
Recife
Salvador
(Bahia)

EQUATOR
10°N
0°
10°S
40°W
50°W
60°W
70°W
80°W

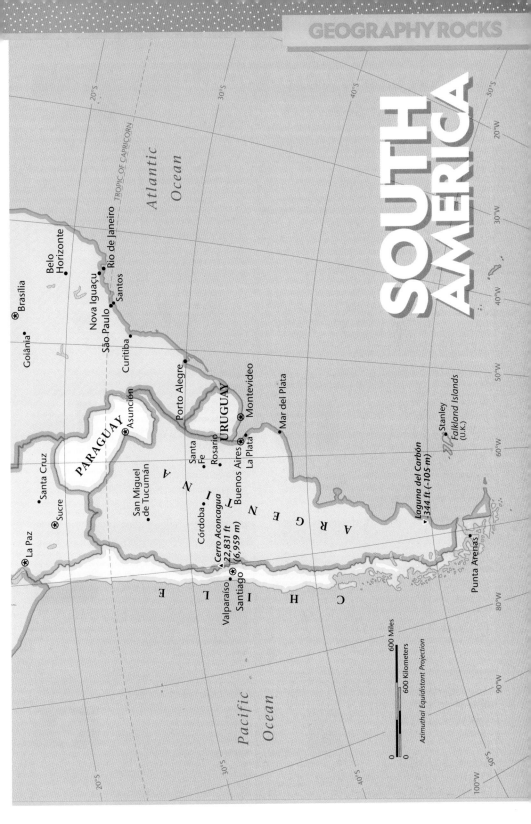

SOUTH AMERICA

Atlantic Ocean

Pacific Ocean

TROPIC OF CAPRICORN

La Paz
Sucre
Santa Cruz
Brasília
Goiânia
Belo Horizonte
Rio de Janeiro
Nova Iguaçu
São Paulo
Santos
Curitiba
Porto Alegre
PARAGUAY
Asunción
URUGUAY
Montevideo
Mar del Plata
Santa Fe
Rosario
Buenos Aires
La Plata
San Miguel de Tucumán
Córdoba
ARGENTINA
Cerro Aconcagua
22,831 ft
(6,959 m)
Valparaíso
Santiago
CHILE
Laguna del Carbón
–344 ft (–105 m)
Stanley
Falkland Islands
(U.K.)
Punta Arenas

20°S
30°S
40°S
50°S

20°W
30°W
40°W
50°W
60°W
70°W
80°W
90°W
100°W
40°S
30°S
20°S

600 Miles
600 Kilometers
Azimuthal Equidistant Projection
0
0

291

COUNTRIES OF THE WORLD

The following pages present a general overview of all 195 independent countries recognized by the National Geographic Society, including the newest nation, South Sudan, which gained independence in 2011.

The flags of each independent country symbolize diverse cultures and histories. The statistical data cover highlights of geography and demography and provide a brief overview of each country. They present general characteristics and are not intended to be comprehensive. For example, not every language spoken in a specific country can be listed. Thus, languages shown are the most representative of that area. This is also true of the religions mentioned.

A country is defined as a political body with its own independent government, geographical space, and, in most cases, laws, military, and taxes.

Disputed areas such as Northern Cyprus and Taiwan, and dependencies of independent nations, such as Bermuda and Puerto Rico, are not included in this listing.

Note the color key at the bottom of the pages and the locator map below, which assign a color to each country based on the continent on which it is located. Some capital city populations include that city's metro area. All information is accurate as of press time.

Color Key by Continent

Afghanistan

Area: 251,773 sq mi (652,090 sq km)
Population: 36,500,000
Capital: Kabul, pop. 4,012,000
Currency: afghani
Religions: Sunni Muslim, Shiite Muslim
Languages: Afghan Persian (Dari), Pashto, Turkic languages (primarily Uzbek and Turkmen), Baluchi, 30 minor languages (including Pashai)

Albania

Area: 11,100 sq mi (28,748 sq km)
Population: 2,900,000
Capital: Tirana, pop. 476,000
Currency: lek
Religions: Muslim, Albanian Orthodox, Roman Catholic
Languages: Albanian, Greek, Vlach, Romani, Slavic dialects

Algeria

Area: 919,595 sq mi (2,381,741 sq km)
Population: 42,700,000
Capital: Algiers, pop. 2,694,000
Currency: Algerian dinar
Religion: Sunni Muslim
Languages: Arabic, French, Berber dialects

Andorra

Area: 181 sq mi (469 sq km)
Population: 80,000
Capital: Andorra la Vella, pop. 23,000
Currency: euro
Religion: Roman Catholic
Languages: Catalan, French, Castilian, Portuguese

Angola

Area: 481,354 sq mi (1,246,700 sq km)
Population: 30,400,000
Capital: Luanda, pop. 7,774,000
Currency: kwanza
Religions: indigenous beliefs, Roman Catholic, Protestant
Languages: Portuguese, Bantu, other African languages

Antigua and Barbuda

Area: 171 sq mi (442 sq km)
Population: 100,000
Capital: St. John's, pop. 21,000
Currency: East Caribbean dollar
Religions: Anglican, Seventh-day Adventist, Pentecostal, Moravian, Roman Catholic, Methodist, Baptist, Church of God, other Christian
Languages: English, local dialects

Argentina

Area: 1,073,518 sq mi
(2,780,400 sq km)
Population: 44,500,000
Capital: Buenos Aires,
pop. 14,967,000
Currency: Argentine peso
Religion: Roman Catholic
Languages: Spanish, English, Italian, German, French

Armenia

Area: 11,484 sq mi
(29,743 sq km)
Population: 3,000,000
Capital: Yerevan,
pop. 1,080,000
Currency: dram
Religions: Armenian Apostolic, other Christian
Language: Armenian

3 cool things about ARMENIA

1. As the first country in the world to adopt Christianity as a state religion, Armenia earns its nickname, "Land of Churches," for its many places of worship. Some still-standing churches date back thousands of years.

2. A 5,500-year-old leather shoe—considered the oldest—was found in an Armenian cave. It looked like a moccasin and was stuffed with grasses.

3. The town of Yerevan is also known as the "Pink City" because many of its buildings and homes are made from a blush-colored volcanic rock.

Australia

Area: 2,988,901 sq mi
(7,741,220 sq km)
Population: 24,100,000
Capital: Canberra, A.C.T.,
pop. 448,000
Currency: Australian dollar
Religions: Roman Catholic, Anglican
Language: English

Austria

Area: 32,378 sq mi (83,858 sq km)
Population: 8,800,000
Capital: Vienna, pop. 1,901,000
Currency: euro
Religions: Roman Catholic, Protestant, Muslim
Language: German

Azerbaijan

Area: 33,436 sq mi
(86,600 sq km)
Population: 9,900,000
Capital: Baku, pop. 2,286,000
Currency: Azerbaijani manat
Religion: Muslim
Language: Azerbaijani (Azeri)

Bahamas

Area: 5,382 sq mi
(13,939 sq km)
Population: 400,000
Capital: Nassau, pop. 280,000
Currency: Bahamian dollar
Religions: Baptist, Anglican, Roman Catholic, Pentecostal, Church of God
Languages: English, Creole

Bahrain

Area: 277 sq mi (717 sq km)
Population: 1,500,000
Capital: Manama, pop. 565,000
Currency: Bahraini dinar
Religions: Shiite Muslim, Sunni Muslim, Christian
Languages: Arabic, English, Farsi, Urdu

Bangladesh

Area: 55,598 sq mi
(143,998 sq km)
Population: 166,400,000
Capital: Dhaka, pop. 19,578,000
Currency: taka
Religions: Muslim, Hindu
Languages: Bangla (Bengali), English

● Asia ● Europe ● North America ● **South America**

Barbados

Area: 166 sq mi (430 sq km)
Population: 300,000
Capital: Bridgetown, pop. 89,000
Currency: Barbadian dollar
Religions: Anglican, Pentecostal, Methodist, other Protestant, Roman Catholic
Language: English

Belarus

Area: 80,153 sq mi (207,595 sq km)
Population: 9,500,000
Capital: Minsk, pop. 2,005,000
Currency: Belarusian ruble
Religions: Eastern Orthodox, other (includes Roman Catholic, Protestant, Jewish, Muslim)
Languages: Belarusian, Russian

Belgium
Area: 11,787 sq mi (30,528 sq km)
Population: 11,400,000
Capital: Brussels, pop. 2,050,000
Currency: euro
Religions: Roman Catholic, other (includes Protestant)
Languages: Dutch, French

Belize
Area: 8,867 sq mi (22,965 sq km)
Population: 400,000
Capital: Belmopan, pop. 23,000
Currency: Belizean dollar
Religions: Roman Catholic, Protestant (includes Pentecostal, Seventh-day Adventist, Mennonite, Methodist)
Languages: Spanish, Creole, Mayan dialects, English, Garifuna (Carib), German

Benin

Area: 43,484 sq mi (112,622 sq km)
Population: 11,500,000
Capitals: Porto-Novo, pop. 285,000; Cotonou, pop. 685,000
Currency: Communauté Financière Africaine franc
Religions: Christian, Muslim, Vodoun
Languages: French, Fon, Yoruba, tribal languages

Bhutan
Area: 17,954 sq mi (46,500 sq km)
Population: 800,000
Capital: Thimphu, pop. 203,000
Currencies: ngultrum; Indian rupee
Religions: Lamaistic Buddhist, Indian- and Nepalese-influenced Hindu
Languages: Dzongkha, Tibetan dialects, Nepalese dialects

Bolivia
Area: 424,164 sq mi (1,098,581 sq km)
Population: 11,300,000
Capitals: La Paz, pop. 1,814,000; Sucre, pop. 278,000
Currency: boliviano
Religions: Roman Catholic, Protestant (includes Evangelical Methodist)
Languages: Spanish, Quechua, Aymara

Bosnia and Herzegovina
Area: 19,741 sq mi (51,129 sq km)
Population: 3,500,000
Capital: Sarajevo, pop. 343,000
Currency: konvertibilna marka (convertible mark)
Religions: Muslim, Orthodox, Roman Catholic
Languages: Bosnian, Croatian, Serbian

Botswana
Area: 224,607 sq mi (581,730 sq km)
Population: 2,200,000
Capital: Gaborone, pop. 269,000
Currency: pula
Religions: Christian, Badimo
Languages: Setswana, Kalanga

Brazil

Area: 3,287,612 sq mi (8,514,877 sq km)
Population: 209,400,000
Capital: Brasília, pop. 4,470,000
Currency: real
Religions: Roman Catholic, Protestant
Language: Portuguese

Brunei

Area: 2,226 sq mi (5,765 sq km)
Population: 400,000
Capital: Bandar Seri Begawan, pop. 41,000
Currency: Bruneian dollar
Religions: Muslim, Buddhist, Christian, other (includes indigenous beliefs)
Languages: Malay, English, Chinese

Burkina Faso

Area: 105,869 sq mi (274,200 sq km)
Population: 20,300,000
Capital: Ouagadougou, pop. 2,531,000
Currency: Communauté Financière Africaine franc
Religions: Muslim, indigenous beliefs, Christian
Languages: French, native African languages

Bulgaria

Area: 42,855 sq mi (110,994 sq km)
Population: 7,000,000
Capital: Sofia, pop. 1,272,000
Currency: lev
Religions: Bulgarian Orthodox, Muslim
Languages: Bulgarian, Turkish, Roma

Burundi

Area: 10,747 sq mi (27,834 sq km)
Population: 11,800,000
Capital: Bujumbura, pop. 899,000
Currency: Burundi franc
Religions: Roman Catholic, indigenous beliefs, Muslim, Protestant
Languages: Kirundi, French, Swahili

SNAPSHOT Bulgaria

Traditional clothing is worn during the Festival of the National Costume in Zheravna, Bulgaria.

● Asia ● Europe ● North America ● South America

Cabo Verde

Area: 1,558 sq mi (4,036 sq km)
Population: 600,000
Capital: Praia, pop. 168,000
Currency: Cape Verdean escudo
Religions: Roman Catholic (infused with indigenous beliefs), Protestant (mostly Church of the Nazarene)
Languages: Portuguese, Crioulo

Cameroon

Area: 183,569 sq mi (475,442 sq km)
Population: 25,600,000
Capital: Yaoundé, pop. 3,656,000
Currency: Communauté Financière Africaine franc
Religions: indigenous beliefs, Christian, Muslim
Languages: 24 major African language groups, English, French

Cambodia

Area: 69,898 sq mi (181,035 sq km)
Population: 16,000,000
Capital: Phnom Penh, pop. 1,952,000
Currency: riel
Religion: Theravada Buddhist
Language: Khmer

Canada

Area: 3,855,103 sq mi (9,984,670 sq km)
Population: 37,200,000
Capital: Ottawa, pop. 1,363,000
Currency: Canadian dollar
Religions: Roman Catholic, Protestant (includes United Church, Anglican), other Christian
Languages: English, French

SNAPSHOT
Colombia

A long-tailed sylph hummingbird feeds on a tropical flower in Colombia.

COLOR KEY ● Africa ● Australia, New Zealand, and Oceania

Central African Republic

Area: 240,535 sq mi
(622,984 sq km)
Population: 4,700,000
Capital: Bangui, pop. 851,000
Currency: Communauté Financière Africaine franc
Religions: indigenous beliefs, Protestant, Roman Catholic, Muslim
Languages: French, Sangho, tribal languages

Chad

Area: 495,755 sq mi
(1,284,000 sq km)
Population: 15,400,000
Capital: N'Djamena, pop. 1,323,000
Currency: Communauté Financière Africaine franc
Religions: Muslim, Catholic, Protestant, animist
Languages: French, Arabic, Sara, more than 120 languages and dialects

Chile

Area: 291,930 sq mi
(756,096 sq km)
Population: 18,600,000
Capital: Santiago, pop. 6,680,000
Currency: Chilean peso
Religions: Roman Catholic, Evangelical
Language: Spanish

China

Area: 3,705,406 sq mi
(9,596,960 sq km)
Population: 1,393,800,000
Capital: Beijing, pop. 19,618,000
Currency: renminbi (yuan)
Religions: Taoist, Buddhist, Christian
Languages: Standard Chinese or Mandarin, Yue, Wu, Minbei, Minnan, Xiang, Gan, Hakka dialects

Colombia

Area: 440,831 sq mi
(1,141,748 sq km)
Population: 49,800,000
Capital: Bogotá, pop. 10,574,000
Currency: Colombian peso
Religion: Roman Catholic
Language: Spanish

Comoros

Area: 863 sq mi (2,235 sq km)
Population: 800,000
Capital: Moroni, pop. 62,000
Currency: Comoran franc
Religion: Sunni Muslim
Languages: Arabic, French, Shikomoro

Congo

Area: 132,047 sq mi (342,000 sq km)
Population: 5,400,000
Capital: Brazzaville, pop. 2,230,000
Currency: Communauté Financière Africaine franc
Religions: Christian, animist
Languages: French, Lingala, Monokutuba, local languages

Costa Rica

Area: 19,730 sq mi
(51,100 sq km)
Population: 5,000,000
Capital: San José, pop. 1,358,000
Currency: Costa Rican colón
Religions: Roman Catholic, Evangelical
Languages: Spanish, English

Côte d'Ivoire (Ivory Coast)

Area: 124,503 sq mi
(322,462 sq km)
Population: 24,900,000
Capitals: Abidjan, pop. 4,921,000; Yamoussoukro, pop. 231,000
Currency: Communauté Financière Africaine franc
Religions: Muslim, indigenous beliefs, Christian
Languages: French, Dioula, other native dialects

Croatia

Area: 21,831 sq mi
(56,542 sq km)
Population: 4,100,000
Capital: Zagreb, pop. 686,000
Currency: kuna
Religions: Roman Catholic, Orthodox
Language: Croatian

Cuba

Area: 42,803 sq mi
(110,860 sq km)
Population: 11,100,000
Capital: Havana, pop. 2,136,000
Currency: Cuban peso
Religions: Roman Catholic, Protestant, Jehovah's Witnesses, Jewish, Santería
Language: Spanish

3 cool things about CUBA

1. The world's smallest bird, the bee hummingbird, inhabits Cuba's Isla de la Juventud. The tiny birds, which grow to be about the size of the insect they're named for, build nests the size of quarters and lay pea-size eggs.

2. The national sport of Cuba is baseball, which was brought to the country in the 1860s. Today, the country has one of the top national teams in the world and many major league players come from Cuba.

3. Cuba is nicknamed *El Cocodrilo* (Spanish for crocodile), after the shape of the island. It's also home to some 3,000 Cuban crocodiles, a critically endangered species that can grow to be almost as long as a full-size car.

Cyprus

Area: 3,572 sq mi (9,251 sq km)
Population: 1,200,000
Capital: Nicosia, pop. 269,000
Currencies: euro; new Turkish lira in Northern Cyprus
Religions: Greek Orthodox, Muslim, Maronite, Armenian Apostolic
Languages: Greek, Turkish, English

Czechia (Czech Republic)

Area: 30,450 sq mi (78,866 sq km)
Population: 10,600,000
Capital: Prague, pop. 1,292,000
Currency: koruny
Religion: Roman Catholic
Language: Czech

Democratic Republic of the Congo

Area: 905,365 sq mi
(2,344,885 sq km)
Population: 84,300,000
Capital: Kinshasa, pop. 13,171,000
Currency: Congolese franc
Religions: Roman Catholic, Protestant, Kimbanguist, Muslim, syncretic sects, indigenous beliefs
Languages: French, Lingala, Kingwana, Kikongo, Tshiluba

Denmark

Area: 16,640 sq mi (43,098 sq km)
Population: 5,800,000
Capital: Copenhagen, pop. 1,321,000
Currency: Danish krone
Religions: Evangelical Lutheran, other Protestant, Roman Catholic
Languages: Danish, Faroese, Greenlandic, German, English as second language

Djibouti

Area: 8,958 sq mi
(23,200 sq km)
Population: 1,000,000
Capital: Djibouti, pop. 562,000
Currency: Djiboutian franc
Religions: Muslim, Christian
Languages: French, Arabic, Somali, Afar

Dominica

Area: 290 sq mi (751 sq km)
Population: 70,000
Capital: Roseau, pop. 15,000
Currency: East Caribbean dollar
Religions: Roman Catholic, Seventh-day Adventist, Pentecostal, Baptist, Methodist, other Christian
Languages: English, French patois

Dominican Republic

Area: 18,704 sq mi
(48,442 sq km)
Population: 10,800,000
Capital: Santo Domingo, pop. 3,172,000
Currency: Dominican peso
Religion: Roman Catholic
Language: Spanish

Ecuador

Area: 109,483 sq mi (283,560 sq km)
Population: 17,000,000
Capital: Quito, pop. 1,822,000
Currency: U.S. dollar
Religion: Roman Catholic
Languages: Spanish, Quechua, other Amerindian languages

Egypt

Area: 386,874 sq mi (1,002,000 sq km)
Population: 97,000,000
Capital: Cairo, pop. 20,901,000
Currency: Egyptian pound
Religions: Muslim (mostly Sunni), Coptic Christian
Languages: Arabic, English, French

El Salvador

Area: 8,124 sq mi (21,041 sq km)
Population: 6,500,000
Capital: San Salvador, pop. 1,107,000
Currency: U.S. dollar
Religions: Roman Catholic, Protestant
Languages: Spanish, Nahua

Equatorial Guinea

Area: 10,831 sq mi (28,051 sq km)
Population: 1,300,000
Capital: Malabo, pop. 297,000
Currency: Communauté Financière Africaine franc
Religions: Christian (predominantly Roman Catholic), pagan practices
Languages: Spanish, French, Fang, Bubi

Eritrea

Area: 45,406 sq mi (117,600 sq km)
Population: 6,000,000
Capital: Asmara, pop. 896,000
Currency: nakfa
Religions: Muslim, Coptic Christian, Roman Catholic
Languages: Afar, Arabic, Tigre, Kunama, Tigrinya, other Cushitic languages

Estonia
Area: 17,462 sq mi (45,227 sq km)
Population: 1,300,000
Capital: Tallinn, pop. 437,000
Currency: euro
Religions: Evangelical Lutheran, Orthodox
Languages: Estonian, Russian

Eswatini

Area: 6,704 sq mi (17,363 sq km)
Population: 1,400,000
Capitals: Mbabane, pop. 68,000; Lobamba, pop. 11,000
Currency: lilangeni
Religions: Zionist, Roman Catholic, Muslim
Languages: English, siSwati

Ethiopia

Area: 426,373 sq mi (1,104,300 sq km)
Population: 107,500,000
Capital: Addis Ababa, pop. 4,400,000
Currency: birr
Religions: Christian, Muslim, traditional
Languages: Amharic, Oromigna, Tigrinya, Guaragigna

Fiji

Area: 7,095 sq mi (18,376 sq km)
Population: 900,000
Capital: Suva, pop. 178,000
Currency: Fijian dollar
Religions: Christian (Methodist, Roman Catholic, Assembly of God), Hindu (Sanatan), Muslim (Sunni)
Languages: English, Fijian, Hindustani

Finland

Area: 130,558 sq mi (338,145 sq km)
Population: 5,500,000
Capital: Helsinki, pop. 1,279,000
Currency: euro
Religion: Lutheran Church of Finland
Languages: Finnish, Swedish

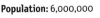
● Asia ● Europe ● North America ● South America

299

France

Area: 210,026 sq mi (543,965 sq km)
Population: 65,100,000
Capital: Paris, pop. 10,901,000
Currency: euro
Religions: Roman Catholic, Muslim
Language: French

Gambia

Area: 4,361 sq mi (11,295 sq km)
Population: 2,200,000
Capital: Banjul, pop. 437,000
Currency: dalasi
Religions: Muslim, Christian
Languages: English, Mandinka, Wolof, Fula, other indigenous vernaculars

Gabon

Area: 103,347 sq mi (267,667 sq km)
Population: 2,100,000
Capital: Libreville, pop. 813,000
Currency: Communauté Financière Africaine franc
Religions: Christian, animist
Languages: French, Fang, Myene, Nzebi, Bapounou/Eschira, Bandjabi

Georgia

Area: 26,911 sq mi (69,700 sq km)
Population: 3,900,000
Capital: Tbilisi, pop. 1,077,000
Currency: lari
Religions: Orthodox Christian, Muslim, Armenian-Gregorian
Languages: Georgian, Russian, Armenian, Azeri, Abkhaz

SNAPSHOT Georgia

Tbilisi, Georgia

Germany

Area: 137,847 sq mi
(357,022 sq km)
Population: 82,800,000
Capital: Berlin, pop. 3,552,000
Currency: euro
Religions: Protestant, Roman Catholic, Muslim
Language: German

Guinea

Area: 94,926 sq mi (245,857 sq km)
Population: 11,900,000
Capital: Conakry, pop. 1,843,000
Currency: Guinean franc
Religions: Muslim, Christian, indigenous beliefs
Languages: French, ethnic languages

Ghana

Area: 92,100 sq mi (238,537 sq km)
Population: 29,500,000
Capital: Accra, pop. 2,439,000
Currency: Ghana cedi
Religions: Christian (Pentecostal/Charismatic, Protestant, Roman Catholic, other), Muslim, traditional beliefs
Languages: Asante, Ewe, Fante, Boron (Brong), Dagomba, Dangme, Dagarte (Dagaba), Akyem, Ga, English

Guinea-Bissau

Area: 13,948 sq mi
(36,125 sq km)
Population: 1,900,000
Capital: Bissau, pop. 558,000
Currency: Communauté
Financière Africaine franc
Religions: indigenous beliefs, Muslim, Christian
Languages: Portuguese, Crioulo, African languages

Greece

Area: 50,949 sq mi (131,957 sq km)
Population: 10,600,000
Capital: Athens, pop. 3,156,000
Currency: euro
Religion: Greek Orthodox
Languages: Greek, English, French

Guyana

Area: 83,000 sq mi
(214,969 sq km)
Population: 800,000
Capital: Georgetown, pop. 110,000
Currency: Guyanese dollar
Religions: Christian, Hindu, Muslim
Languages: English, Amerindian dialects, Creole, Hindustani, Urdu

Grenada

Area: 133 sq mi (344 sq km)
Population: 100,000
Capital: St. George's, pop. 39,000
Currency: East Caribbean dollar
Religions: Roman Catholic, Anglican, other Protestant
Languages: English, French patois

Haiti

Area: 10,714 sq mi (27,750 sq km)
Population: 10,800,000
Capital: Port-au-Prince,
pop. 2,637,000
Currency: gourde
Religions: Roman Catholic, Protestant (Baptist, Pentecostal, other)
Languages: French, Creole

Guatemala

Area: 42,042 sq mi (108,889 sq km)
Population: 17,200,000
Capital: Guatemala City,
pop. 2,851,000
Currency: quetzal
Religions: Roman Catholic, Protestant, indigenous Maya beliefs
Languages: Spanish, 23 official Amerindian languages

Honduras

Area: 43,433 sq mi
(112,492 sq km)
Population: 9,000,000
Capital: Tegucigalpa,
pop. 1,363,000
Currency: lempira
Religions: Roman Catholic, Protestant
Languages: Spanish, Amerindian dialects

Hungary

Area: 35,919 sq mi (93,030 sq km)
Population: 9,800,000
Capital: Budapest, pop. 1,759,000
Currency: forint
Religions: Roman Catholic, Calvinist, Lutheran
Language: Hungarian

Iraq

Area: 168,754 sq mi
(437,072 sq km)
Population: 40,200,000
Capital: Baghdad, pop. 6,812,000
Currency: Iraqi dinar
Religions: Shiite Muslim, Sunni Muslim
Languages: Arabic, Kurdish, Assyrian, Armenian

Iceland

Area: 39,769 sq mi
(103,000 sq km)
Population: 400,000
Capital: Reykjavík, pop. 216,000
Currency: Icelandic krona
Religion: Lutheran Church of Iceland
Languages: Icelandic, English, Nordic
languages, German

Ireland (Éire)

Area: 27,133 sq mi
(70,273 sq km)
Population: 4,900,000
Capital: Dublin, pop. 1,201,000
Currency: euro
Religions: Roman Catholic, Church of Ireland
Languages: Irish (Gaelic), English

India

Area: 1,269,221 sq mi (3,287,270 sq km)
Population: 1,371,300,000
Capital: New Delhi, pop. 28,514,000
(part of Delhi metropolitan area)
Currency: Indian rupee
Religions: Hindu, Muslim
Languages: Hindi, 21 other official languages,
Hindustani (popular Hindi/Urdu variant in the north)

Israel

Area: 8,550 sq mi (22,145 sq km)
Population: 8,500,000
Capital: Jerusalem, pop. 907,000
Currency: new Israeli sheqel
Religions: Jewish, Muslim
Languages: Hebrew, Arabic, English

Indonesia

Area: 742,308 sq mi
(1,922,570 sq km)
Population: 265,200,000
Capital: Jakarta, pop. 10,517,000
Currency: Indonesian rupiah
Religions: Muslim, Protestant, Roman Catholic
Languages: Bahasa Indonesia (modified form of Malay),
English, Dutch, Javanese, local dialects

Italy

Area: 116,345 sq mi
(301,333 sq km)
Population: 60,600,000
Capital: Rome, pop. 4,210,000
Currency: euro
Religions: Roman Catholic, Protestant, Jewish, Muslim
Languages: Italian, German, French, Slovene

Iran

Area: 636,296 sq mi
(1,648,000 sq km)
Population: 81,600,000
Capital: Tehran, pop. 8,896,000
Currency: Iranian rial
Religions: Shiite Muslim, Sunni Muslim
Languages: Persian, Turkic, Kurdish, Luri,
Baluchi, Arabic

Jamaica

Area: 4,244 sq mi
(10,991 sq km)
Population: 2,900,000
Capital: Kingston, pop. 589,000
Currency: Jamaican dollar
Religions: Protestant (Church of God, Seventh-day
Adventist, Pentecostal, Baptist, Anglican, other)
Languages: English, English patois

Japan

Area: 145,902 sq mi (377,887 sq km)
Population: 126,500,000
Capital: Tokyo, pop. 37,393,000
Currency: yen
Religions: Shinto, Buddhist
Language: Japanese

Kazakhstan

Area: 1,049,155 sq mi (2,717,300 sq km)
Population: 18,400,000
Capital: Astana, pop. 1,068,000
Currency: tenge
Religions: Muslim, Russian Orthodox
Languages: Kazakh (Qazaq), Russian

Jordan

Area: 34,495 sq mi (89,342 sq km)
Population: 10,200,000
Capital: Amman, pop. 2,065,000
Currency: Jordanian dinar
Religions: Sunni Muslim, Christian
Languages: Arabic, English

Kenya

Area: 224,081 sq mi (580,367 sq km)
Population: 51,000,000
Capital: Nairobi, pop. 4,386,000
Currency: Kenyan shilling
Religions: Protestant, Roman Catholic, Muslim, indigenous beliefs
Languages: English, Kiswahili, many indigenous languages

SNAPSHOT
Jamaica

Children dance in Kingston, Jamaica, wearing yellow, green, and black— Jamaica's national colors.

● Asia   ● Europe   ● North America   ● **South America**

Kiribati

Area: 313 sq mi (811 sq km)
Population: 100,000
Capital: Tarawa, pop. 64,000
Currency: Australian dollar
Religions: Roman Catholic, Protestant (Congregational)
Languages: I-Kiribati, English

Kuwait

Area: 6,880 sq mi (17,818 sq km)
Population: 4,200,000
Capital: Kuwait City, pop. 2,989,000
Currency: Kuwaiti dinar
Religions: Sunni Muslim, Shiite Muslim
Languages: Arabic, English

Kosovo

Area: 4,203 sq mi (10,887 sq km)
Population: 1,800,000
Capital: Pristina, pop. 205,000
Currency: euro
Religions: Muslim, Serbian Orthodox, Roman Catholic
Languages: Albanian, Serbian, Bosnian, Turkish, Roma

Kyrgyzstan

Area: 77,182 sq mi (199,900 sq km)
Population: 6,100,000
Capital: Bishkek, pop. 996,000
Currency: som
Religions: Muslim, Russian Orthodox
Languages: Kyrgyz, Uzbek, Russian

SNAPSHOT
Luxembourg

Pretzel from Grevenmacher, Luxembourg

COLOR KEY ● Africa ● Australia, New Zealand, and Oceania

Laos

Area: 91,429 sq mi
(236,800 sq km)
Population: 7,000,000
Capital: Vientiane, pop. 665,000
Currency: kip
Religions: Buddhist, animist
Languages: Lao, French, English, various ethnic languages

Libya

Area: 679,362 sq mi
(1,759,540 sq km)
Population: 6,500,000
Capital: Tripoli, pop. 1,158,000
Currency: Libyan dinar
Religion: Sunni Muslim
Languages: Arabic, Italian, English

Latvia

Area: 24,938 sq mi
(64,589 sq km)
Population: 1,900,000
Capital: Riga, pop. 637,000
Currency: Latvian lat
Religions: Lutheran, Roman Catholic, Russian Orthodox
Languages: Latvian, Russian, Lithuanian

Liechtenstein

Area: 62 sq mi (160 sq km)
Population: 40,000
Capital: Vaduz, pop. 5,000
Currency: Swiss franc
Religions: Roman Catholic, Protestant
Languages: German, Alemannic dialect

Lebanon

Area: 4,036 sq mi (10,452 sq km)
Population: 6,100,000
Capital: Beirut, pop. 2,385,000
Currency: Lebanese pound
Religions: Muslim, Christian
Languages: Arabic, French, English, Armenian

Lithuania

Area: 25,212 sq mi
(65,300 sq km)
Population: 2,800,000
Capital: Vilnius, pop. 536,000
Currency: litas
Religions: Roman Catholic, Russian Orthodox
Languages: Lithuanian, Russian, Polish

Lesotho

Area: 11,720 sq mi (30,355 sq km)
Population: 2,300,000
Capital: Maseru, pop. 202,000
Currencies: loti; South African rand
Religions: Christian, indigenous beliefs
Languages: Sesotho, English, Zulu, Xhosa

Luxembourg

Area: 998 sq mi (2,586 sq km)
Population: 600,000
Capital: Luxembourg,
pop. 120,000
Currency: euro
Religions: Roman Catholic, Protestant, Jewish, Muslim
Languages: Luxembourgish, German, French

Liberia

Area: 43,000 sq mi
(111,370 sq km)
Population: 4,900,000
Capital: Monrovia,
pop. 1,418,000
Currency: Liberian dollar
Religions: Christian, indigenous beliefs, Muslim
Languages: English, some 20 ethnic languages

Macedonia

Area: 9,928 sq mi
(25,713 sq km)
Population: 2,100,000
Capital: Skopje, pop. 584,000
Currency: Macedonian denar
Religions: Macedonian Orthodox, Muslim
Languages: Macedonian, Albanian, Turkish

Madagascar

Area: 226,658 sq mi
(587,041 sq km)
Population: 26,300,000
Capital: Antananarivo,
pop. 3,058,000
Currency: Madagascar ariary
Religions: indigenous beliefs, Christian, Muslim
Languages: English, French, Malagasy

Malawi

Area: 45,747 sq mi
(118,484 sq km)
Population: 19,100,000
Capital: Lilongwe, pop. 1,030,000
Currency: Malawian kwacha
Religions: Christian, Muslim
Languages: Chichewa, Chinyanja, Chiyao, Chitumbuka

Malaysia

Area: 127,355 sq mi (329,847 sq km)
Population: 32,500,000
Capital: Kuala Lumpur,
pop. 7,564,000
Currency: ringgit
Religions: Muslim, Buddhist, Christian, Hindu
Languages: Bahasa Malaysia, English, Chinese, Tamil,
Telugu, Malayalam, Panjabi, Thai, indigenous languages

Maldives

Area: 115 sq mi (298 sq km)
Population: 400,000
Capital: Male, pop. 177,000
Currency: rufiyaa
Religion: Sunni Muslim
Languages: Maldivian Dhivehi, English

Mali

Area: 478,841 sq mi (1,240,192 sq km)
Population: 19,400,000
Capital: Bamako, pop. 2,447,000
Currency: Communauté
Financière Africaine franc
Religions: Muslim, indigenous beliefs
Languages: Bambara, French, numerous
African languages

Malta

Area: 122 sq mi (316 sq km)
Population: 500,000
Capital: Valletta, pop. 213,000
Currency: euro
Religion: Roman Catholic
Languages: Maltese, English

Marshall Islands

Area: 70 sq mi (181 sq km)
Population: 60,000
Capital: Majuro, pop. 31,000
Currency: U.S. dollar
Religions: Protestant, Assembly of God,
Roman Catholic
Language: Marshallese

Mauritania

Area: 397,955 sq mi
(1,030,700 sq km)
Population: 4,500,000
Capital: Nouakchott, pop. 1,205,000
Currency: ouguiya
Religion: Muslim
Languages: Arabic, Pulaar, Soninke, French,
Hassaniya, Wolof

3 cool things about MAURITANIA

1. Nouakchott was designated as Mauritania's
capital when the country gained independence
in 1960, making it one of the world's newest
capitals. Once a tiny fishing village, Nouakchott
is now the country's largest city.

2. "The Eye of Africa"—a 30-mile (50-km)-wide
bull's-eye rock formation in the Sahara in
Mauritania can be seen from space. The
natural phenomenon was likely formed by
geological shifts and exposed over time
by wind and water erosion.

3. The rusty remains of some 300 ships once
bobbed along in Mauritania's Bay of
Nouadhibou. It was one of the world's biggest
ship cemeteries, and boats from all over the
world were abandoned there during the 1980s.

Mauritius

Area: 788 sq mi (2,040 sq km)
Population: 1,300,000
Capital: Port Louis, pop. 149,000
Currency: Mauritian rupee
Religions: Hindu, Roman Catholic, Muslim, other Christian
Languages: Creole, Bhojpuri, French

Mexico

Area: 758,449 sq mi (1,964,375 sq km)
Population: 130,800,000
Capital: Mexico City, pop. 21,782,000
Currency: Mexican peso
Religions: Roman Catholic, Protestant
Languages: Spanish, Mayan, other indigenous languages

Micronesia

Area: 271 sq mi (702 sq km)
Population: 100,000
Capital: Palikir, pop. 7,000
Currency: U.S. dollar
Religions: Roman Catholic, Protestant
Languages: English, Trukese, Pohnpeian, Yapese, other indigenous languages

Moldova

Area: 13,050 sq mi (33,800 sq km)
Population: 3,500,000
Capital: Chișinău, pop. 510,000
Currency: Moldovan leu
Religion: Eastern Orthodox
Languages: Moldovan, Russian, Gagauz

Monaco

Area: 0.8 sq mi (2 sq km)
Population: 40,000
Capital: Monaco, pop. 39,000
Currency: euro
Religion: Roman Catholic
Languages: French, English, Italian, Monegasque

Mongolia

Area: 603,909 sq mi (1,564,116 sq km)
Population: 3,200,000
Capital: Ulaanbaatar, pop. 1,520,000
Currency: togrog/tugrik
Religions: Buddhist Lamaist, Shamanist, Christian
Languages: Khalkha Mongol, Turkic, Russian

Montenegro

Area: 5,333 sq mi (13,812 sq km)
Population: 600,000
Capital: Podgorica, pop. 177,000
Currency: euro
Religions: Orthodox, Muslim, Roman Catholic
Languages: Serbian (Ijekavian dialect), Bosnian, Albanian, Croatian

MONTENEGRO—WHICH MEANS "BLACK MOUNTAIN"—is home to many DARK MOUNTAIN FORESTS.

Morocco

Area: 172,414 sq mi (446,550 sq km)
Population: 35,200,000
Capital: Rabat, pop. 1,847,000
Currency: Moroccan dirham
Religion: Muslim
Languages: Arabic, Berber dialects, French

Mozambique

Area: 308,642 sq mi (799,380 sq km)
Population: 30,500,000
Capital: Maputo, pop. 1,102,000
Currency: metical
Religions: Roman Catholic, Muslim, Zionist Christian
Languages: Emakhuwa, Xichangana, Portuguese, Elomwe, Cisena, Echuwabo, other local languages

Myanmar (Burma)

Area: 261,218 sq mi
(676,552 sq km)
Population: 53,900,000
Capital: Nay Pyi Taw,
pop. 500,000
Currency: kyat
Religions: Buddhist, Christian, Muslim
Languages: Burmese, minority ethnic languages

Nauru

Area: 8 sq mi (21 sq km)
Population: 11,000
Capital: Yaren, pop. 11,000
Currency: Australian dollar
Religions: Protestant, Roman Catholic
Languages: Nauruan, English

Namibia

Area: 318,261 sq mi
(824,292 sq km)
Population: 2,500,000
Capital: Windhoek, pop. 404,000
Currencies: Namibian dollar;
South African rand
Religions: Lutheran, other Christian, indigenous beliefs
Languages: Afrikaans, German, English

Nepal

Area: 56,827 sq mi
(147,181 sq km)
Population: 29,700,000
Capital: Kathmandu, pop. 1,330,000
Currency: Nepalese rupee
Religions: Hindu, Buddhist, Muslim, Kirant
Languages: Nepali, Maithali, Bhojpuri, Tharu,
Tamang, Newar, Magar

SNAPSHOT
Nepal

A street vendor sells flowers
and vegetables in Patan, Nepal.

COLOR KEY   ● Africa ● Australia, New Zealand, and Oceania

Netherlands

Area: 16,034 sq mi
(41,528 sq km)
Population: 17,200,000
Capital: Amsterdam, pop. 1,132,000;
The Hague, pop. 685,000
Currency: euro
Religions: Roman Catholic, Dutch Reformed,
Calvinist, Muslim
Languages: Dutch, Frisian

New Zealand

Area: 104,454 sq mi
(270,534 sq km)
Population: 4,900,000
Capital: Wellington, pop. 411,000
Currency: New Zealand dollar
Religions: Anglican, Roman Catholic, Presbyterian,
other Christian
Languages: English, Maori

Nicaragua

Area: 50,193 sq mi
(130,000 sq km)
Population: 6,300,000
Capital: Managua, pop. 1,048,000
Currency: gold cordoba
Religions: Roman Catholic, Evangelical
Language: Spanish

Niger

Area: 489,191 sq mi (1,267,000 sq km)
Population: 22,200,000
Capital: Niamey, pop. 1,214,000
Currency: Communauté
Financière Africaine franc
Religions: Muslim, other (includes indigenous
beliefs and Christian)
Languages: French, Hausa, Djerma

Nigeria

Area: 356,669 sq mi
(923,768 sq km)
Population: 195,900,000
Capital: Abuja, pop. 2,919,000
Currency: naira
Religions: Muslim, Christian, indigenous beliefs
Languages: English, Hausa, Yoruba, Igbo (Ibo), Fulani

North Korea

Area: 46,540 sq mi
(120,538 sq km)
Population: 25,600,000
Capital: Pyongyang,
pop. 3,038,000
Currency: North Korean won
Religions: Buddhist, Confucianist, some Christian
and syncretic Chondogyo
Language: Korean

Norway

Area: 125,004 sq mi
(323,758 sq km)
Population: 5,300,000
Capital: Oslo, pop. 1,012,000
Currency: Norwegian krone
Religion: Church of Norway (Lutheran)
Languages: Bokmal Norwegian, Nynorsk
Norwegian, Sami

Oman

Area: 119,500 sq mi
(309,500 sq km)
Population: 4,700,000
Capital: Muscat, pop. 1,447,000
Currency: Omani rial
Religions: Ibadhi Muslim, Sunni Muslim,
Shiite Muslim, Hindu
Languages: Arabic, English, Baluchi, Urdu, Indian dialects

Pakistan

Area: 307,374 sq mi
(796,095 sq km)
Population: 200,600,000
Capital: Islamabad, pop. 1,061,000
Currency: Pakistani rupee
Religions: Sunni Muslim, Shiite Muslim
Languages: Punjabi, Sindhi, Siraiki, Pashto, Urdu,
Baluchi, Hindko, English

Palau

Area: 189 sq mi (489 sq km)
Population: 20,000
Capital: Melekeok, pop. 11,000
Currency: U.S. dollar
Religions: Roman Catholic, Protestant, Modekngei,
Seventh-day Adventist
Languages: Palauan, Filipino, English, Chinese

Panama

Area: 29,157 sq mi (75,517 sq km)
Population: 4,200,000
Capital: Panama City, pop. 1,783,000
Currencies: balboa; U.S. dollar
Religions: Roman Catholic, Protestant
Languages: Spanish, English

Poland

Area: 120,728 sq mi (312,685 sq km)
Population: 38,400,000
Capital: Warsaw, pop. 1,768,000
Currency: zloty
Religion: Roman Catholic
Language: Polish

Papua New Guinea

Area: 178,703 sq mi (462,840 sq km)
Population: 8,500,000
Capital: Port Moresby, pop. 367,000
Currency: kina
Religions: indigenous beliefs, Roman Catholic, Lutheran, other Protestant
Languages: Melanesian Pidgin, 820 indigenous languages

Portugal

Area: 35,655 sq mi (92,345 sq km)
Population: 10,300,000
Capital: Lisbon, pop. 2,927,000
Currency: euro
Religion: Roman Catholic
Languages: Portuguese, Mirandese

Paraguay

Area: 157,048 sq mi (406,752 sq km)
Population: 6,900,000
Capital: Asunción, pop. 3,222,000
Currency: guarani
Religions: Roman Catholic, Protestant
Languages: Spanish, Guarani

Qatar

Area: 4,448 sq mi (11,521 sq km)
Population: 2,700,000
Capital: Doha, pop. 633,000
Currency: Qatari rial
Religions: Muslim, Christian
Languages: Arabic; English commonly a second language

Peru

Area: 496,224 sq mi (1,285,216 sq km)
Population: 32,200,000
Capital: Lima, pop. 10,391,000
Currency: nuevo sol
Religion: Roman Catholic
Languages: Spanish, Quechua, Aymara, minor Amazonian languages

Romania

Area: 92,043 sq mi (238,391 sq km)
Population: 19,500,000
Capital: Bucharest, pop. 1,821,000
Currency: new leu
Religions: Eastern Orthodox, Protestant, Roman Catholic
Languages: Romanian, Hungarian

Philippines

Area: 115,831 sq mi (300,000 sq km)
Population: 107,000,000
Capital: Manila, pop. 13,482,000
Currency: Philippine peso
Religions: Roman Catholic, Muslim, other Christian
Languages: Filipino (based on Tagalog), English

Russia

Area: 6,592,850 sq mi (17,075,400 sq km)
Population: 147,300,000
Capital: Moscow, pop. 12,538,000
Currency: ruble
Religions: Russian Orthodox, Muslim
Languages: Russian, many minority languages

Note: Russia is in both Europe and Asia, but its capital is in Europe, so it is classified here as a European country.

COLOR KEY ● Africa ● Australia, New Zealand, and Oceania

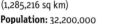

Rwanda

Area: 10,169 sq mi
(26,338 sq km)
Population: 12,600,000
Capital: Kigali, pop. 1,058,000
Currency: Rwandan franc
Religions: Roman Catholic, Protestant, Adventist, Muslim
Languages: Kinyarwanda, French, English, Kiswahili

San Marino

Area: 24 sq mi (61 sq km)
Population: 30,000
Capital: San Marino, pop. 4,000
Currency: euro
Religion: Roman Catholic
Language: Italian

Samoa

Area: 1,093 sq mi (2,831 sq km)
Population: 200,000
Capital: Apia, pop. 36,000
Currency: tala
Religions: Congregationalist, Roman Catholic, Methodist, Church of Jesus Christ of Latter-day Saints, Assembly of God, Seventh-day Adventist
Languages: Samoan (Polynesian), English

Sao Tome and Principe

Area: 386 sq mi (1,001 sq km)
Population: 200,000
Capital: São Tomé, pop. 80,000
Currency: dobra
Religions: Roman Catholic, Evangelical
Language: Portuguese

SNAPSHOT
Papua New Guinea

Children ride in a homemade canoe in Kavieng, New Ireland, Papua New Guinea.

● Asia ● Europe ● North America ● South America

Saudi Arabia

Area: 756,985 sq mi
(1,960,582 sq km)
Population: 33,400,000
Capital: Riyadh, pop. 6,907,000
Currency: Saudi riyal
Religion: Muslim
Language: Arabic

Senegal

Area: 75,955 sq mi
(196,722 sq km)
Population: 16,300,000
Capital: Dakar, pop. 2,978,000
Currency: Communauté
Financière Africaine franc
Religions: Muslim, Christian (mostly Roman Catholic)
Languages: French, Wolof, Pulaar, Jola, Mandinka

Serbia

Area: 29,913 sq mi (77,474 sq km)
Population: 7,000,000
Capital: Belgrade, pop. 1,389,000
Currency: Serbian dinar
Religions: Serbian Orthodox, Roman Catholic, Muslim
Languages: Serbian, Hungarian

Seychelles

Area: 176 sq mi (455 sq km)
Population: 100,000
Capital: Victoria, pop. 28,000
Currency: Seychelles rupee
Religions: Roman Catholic, Anglican, other Christian
Languages: Creole, English

Sierra Leone

Area: 27,699 sq mi (71,740 sq km)
Population: 7,700,000
Capital: Freetown, pop. 1,136,000
Currency: leone
Religions: Muslim, indigenous beliefs, Christian
Languages: English, Mende, Temne, Krio

Singapore

Area: 255 sq mi (660 sq km)
Population: 5,800,000
Capital: Singapore, pop. 5,792,000
Currency: Singapore dollar
Religions: Buddhist, Muslim, Taoist, Roman Catholic, Hindu, other Christian
Languages: Mandarin, English, Malay, Hokkien, Cantonese, Teochew, Tamil

Slovakia

Area: 18,932 sq mi
(49,035 sq km)
Population: 5,400,000
Capital: Bratislava, pop. 430,000
Currency: euro
Religions: Roman Catholic, Protestant, Greek Catholic
Languages: Slovak, Hungarian

Slovenia

Area: 7,827 sq mi
(20,273 sq km)
Population: 2,100,000
Capital: Ljubljana,
pop. 286,000
Currency: euro
Religions: Roman Catholic, Muslim, Orthodox
Languages: Slovene, Croatian, Serbian

3 cool things about SLOVENIA

1. Some 54 percent of Slovenia's land is forest. Kočevje, a town that is made up of about 90 percent forest, is also known as Slovenia's Bear Forest, as it's home to much of the country's 500-strong brown bear population.

2. There are about 10,000 caves in Slovenia, including Postojna Cave, which has 15 miles (24 km) of passages, galleries, and chambers that started forming some three million years ago.

3. A 1,181-foot (360-m)-tall chimney soars above the city of Trbovlje, Slovenia. The tallest chimney in Europe, it's part of the old Trbovlje Power Station and is a destination for climbers, who scale the more than 50-year-old tower.

Solomon Islands

Area: 10,954 sq mi
(28,370 sq km)
Population: 700,000
Capital: Honiara, pop. 82,000
Currency: Solomon Islands dollar
Religions: Church of Melanesia, Roman Catholic,
South Seas Evangelical, other Christian
Languages: Melanesian pidgin, 120 indigenous languages

Somalia

Area: 246,201 sq mi
(637,657 sq km)
Population: 15,200,000
Capital: Mogadishu, pop. 2,082,000
Currency: Somali shilling
Religion: Sunni Muslim
Languages: Somali, Arabic, Italian, English

South Africa

Area: 470,693 sq mi (1,219,090 sq km)
Population: 57,700,000
Capitals: Pretoria (Tshwane),
pop. 2,378,000; Bloemfontein,
pop. 546,000; Cape Town, pop. 4,430,000
Currency: rand
Religions: Zion Christian, Pentecostal, Catholic,
Methodist, Dutch Reformed, Anglican, other Christian
Languages: IsiZulu, IsiXhosa, Afrikaans, Sepedi, English

South Korea

Area: 38,321 sq mi
(99,250 sq km)
Population: 51,800,000
Capital: Seoul, pop. 9,963,000
Currency: South Korean won
Religions: Christian, Buddhist
Languages: Korean, English

South Sudan

Area: 248,777 sq mi
(644,329 sq km)
Population: 13,000,000
Capital: Juba, pop. 369,000
Currency: South Sudan pound
Religions: animist, Christian
Languages: English, Arabic, regional languages
(Dinke, Nuer, Bari, Zande, Shilluk)

Spain

Area: 195,363 sq mi (505,988 sq km)
Population: 46,700,000
Capital: Madrid, pop. 6,497,000
Currency: euro
Religion: Roman Catholic
Languages: Castilian Spanish, Catalan,
Galician, Basque

Sri Lanka

Area: 25,299 sq mi
(65,525 sq km)
Population: 21,700,000
Capitals: Colombo, pop. 600,000;
Sri Jayewardenepura Kotte, pop. 103,000
Currency: Sri Lankan rupee
Religions: Buddhist, Muslim, Hindu, Christian
Languages: Sinhala, Tamil

St. Kitts and Nevis

Area: 104 sq mi (269 sq km)
Population: 50,000
Capital: Basseterre, pop. 14,000
Currency: East Caribbean dollar
Religions: Anglican, other Protestant,
Roman Catholic
Language: English

St. Lucia

Area: 238 sq mi (616 sq km)
Population: 200,000
Capital: Castries, pop. 22,000
Currency: East Caribbean
dollar
Religions: Roman Catholic, Seventh-day Adventist,
Pentecostal
Languages: English, French patois

St. Vincent and the Grenadines

Area: 150 sq mi (389 sq km)
Population: 100,000
Capital: Kingstown, pop. 27,000
Currency: East Caribbean dollar
Religions: Anglican, Methodist, Roman Catholic
Languages: English, French patois

Sudan
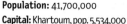

Area: 718,722 sq mi (1,861,484 sq km)
Population: 41,700,000
Capital: Khartoum, pop. 5,534,000
Currency: Sudanese pound
Religions: Sunni Muslim, indigenous beliefs, Christian
Languages: Arabic, Nubian, Ta Bedawie, many diverse dialects of Nilotic, Nilo-Hamitic, Sudanic languages

Suriname

Area: 63,037 sq mi (163,265 sq km)
Population: 600,000
Capital: Paramaribo, pop. 239,000
Currency: Suriname dollar
Religions: Hindu, Protestant (predominantly Moravian), Roman Catholic, Muslim, indigenous beliefs
Languages: Dutch, English, Sranang Tongo, Hindustani, Javanese

Sweden

Area: 173,732 sq mi (449,964 sq km)
Population: 10,200,000
Capital: Stockholm, pop. 1,583,000
Currency: Swedish krona
Religion: Lutheran
Languages: Swedish, Sami, Finnish

Switzerland

Area: 15,940 sq mi (41,284 sq km)
Population: 8,500,000
Capital: Bern, pop. 422,000
Currency: Swiss franc
Religions: Roman Catholic, Protestant, Muslim
Languages: German, French, Italian, Romansh

Syria

Area: 71,498 sq mi (185,180 sq km)
Population: 18,300,000
Capital: Damascus, pop. 2,320,000
Currency: Syrian pound
Religions: Sunni, other Muslim (includes Alawite, Druze), Christian
Languages: Arabic, Kurdish, Armenian, Aramaic, Circassian

Tajikistan

Area: 55,251 sq mi (143,100 sq km)
Population: 9,100,000
Capital: Dushanbe, pop. 873,000
Currency: somoni
Religions: Sunni Muslim, Shiite Muslim
Languages: Tajik, Russian

There's a flag pole as high as a 50-story building in DUSHANBE, TAJIKISTAN.

Tanzania

Area: 364,900 sq mi (945,087 sq km)
Population: 59,100,000
Capitals: Dar es Salaam, pop. 6,048,000; Dodoma, pop. 262,000
Currency: Tanzanian shilling
Religions: Muslim, indigenous beliefs, Christian
Languages: Kiswahili, Kiunguja, English, Arabic, local languages

Thailand

Area: 198,115 sq mi (513,115 sq km)
Population: 66,200,000
Capital: Bangkok, pop. 10,156,000
Currency: baht
Religions: Buddhist, Muslim
Languages: Thai, English, ethnic dialects

Timor-Leste (East Timor)

Area: 5,640 sq mi (14,609 sq km)
Population: 1,200,000
Capital: Dili, pop. 281,000
Currency: U.S. dollar
Religion: Roman Catholic
Languages: Tetum, Portuguese, Indonesian, English, indigenous languages

COLOR KEY ● Africa ● Australia, New Zealand, and Oceania

Togo

Area: 21,925 sq mi (56,785 sq km)
Population: 8,000,000
Capital: Lomé, pop. 1,746,000
Currency: Communauté Financière Africaine franc
Religions: indigenous beliefs, Christian, Muslim
Languages: French, Ewe, Mina, Kabye, Dagomb

Turkey

Area: 300,948 sq mi (779.452 sq km)
Population: 81,300,000
Capital: Ankara, pop. 4,919,000
Currency: new Turkish lira
Religion: Muslim (mostly Sunni)
Languages: Turkish, Kurdish, Dimli (Zaza), Azeri, Kabardian, Gagauz

Tonga

Area: 289 sq mi (748 sq km)
Population: 100,000
Capital: Nuku'alofa, pop. 23,000
Currency: pa'anga
Religion: Christian
Languages: Tongan, English

Turkmenistan

Area: 188,456 sq mi (488,100 sq km)
Population: 5,900,000
Capital: Ashgabat, pop. 810,000
Currency: Turkmen manat
Religions: Muslim, Eastern Orthodox
Languages: Turkmen, Russian, Uzbek

Trinidad and Tobago

Area: 1,980 sq mi (5,128 sq km)
Population: 1,400,000
Capital: Port of Spain, pop. 544,000
Currency: Trinidad and Tobago dollar
Religions: Roman Catholic, Hindu, Anglican, Baptist
Languages: English, Caribbean Hindustani, French, Spanish, Chinese

Tuvalu

Area: 10 sq mi (26 sq km)
Population: 10,000
Capital: Funafuti, pop. 7,000
Currencies: Australian dollar; Tuvaluan dollar
Religion: Church of Tuvalu (Congregationalist)
Languages: Tuvaluan, English, Samoan, Kiribati

LEATHERBACK SEA TURTLES nest on the beaches of TRINIDAD and TOBAGO.

Tuvalu's land area has grown by about 3 PERCENT since the EARLY 1970s.

Tunisia

Area: 63,170 sq mi (163,610 sq km)
Population: 11,600,000
Capital: Tunis, pop. 2,291,000
Currency: Tunisian dinar
Religion: Muslim
Languages: Arabic, French

Uganda

Area: 93,104 sq mi (241,139 sq km)
Population: 44,100,000
Capital: Kampala, pop. 2,986,000
Currency: Ugandan shilling
Religions: Protestant, Roman Catholic, Muslim
Languages: English, Ganda, other local languages, Kiswahili, Arabic

Ukraine

Area: 233,030 sq mi
(603,550 sq km)
Population: 42,300,000
Capital: Kiev, pop. 2,957,000
Currency: hryvnia
Religions: Ukrainian Orthodox, Orthodox, Ukrainian Greek Catholic
Languages: Ukrainian, Russian

United Kingdom

Area: 93,788 sq mi
(242,910 sq km)
Population: 66,400,000
Capital: London, pop. 9,046,000
Currency: British pound
Religions: Anglican, Roman Catholic, Presbyterian, Methodist
Languages: English, Welsh, Scottish form of Gaelic

United Arab Emirates

Area: 30,000 sq mi
(77,700 sq km)
Population: 9,500,000
Capital: Abu Dhabi,
pop. 1,420,000
Currency: Emirati dirham
Religion: Muslim
Languages: Arabic, Persian, English, Hindi, Urdu

United States

Area: 3,794,083 sq mi
(9,826,630 sq km)
Population: 328,000,000
Capital: Washington, D.C.,
pop. 5,207,000
Currency: U.S. dollar
Religions: Protestant, Roman Catholic
Languages: English, Spanish

SNAPSHOT
Zambia

Victoria Falls on the border of Zambia and Zimbabwe

COLOR KEY ● Africa ● Australia, New Zealand, and Oceania

Uruguay

Area: 68,037 sq mi
(176,215 sq km)
Population: 3,500,000
Capital: Montevideo, pop. 1,737,000
Currency: Uruguayan peso
Religion: Roman Catholic
Language: Spanish

There are about FOUR TIMES MORE COWS in Uruguay than people.

Uzbekistan

Area: 172,742 sq mi
(447,400 sq km)
Population: 32,900,000
Capital: Tashkent,
pop. 2,464,000
Currency: Uzbekistani sum
Religions: Muslim (mostly Sunni), Eastern Orthodox
Languages: Uzbek, Russian, Tajik

Vanuatu

Area: 4,707 sq mi (12,190 sq km)
Population: 300,000
Capital: Port Vila, pop. 53,000
Currency: vatu
Religions: Presbyterian, Anglican, Roman Catholic,
other Christian, indigenous beliefs
Languages: more than 100 local languages, pidgin
(known as Bislama or Bichelama)

Vatican City

Area: 0.2 sq mi (0.4 sq km)
Population: 800
Capital: Vatican City, pop. 800
Currency: euro
Religion: Roman Catholic
Languages: Italian, Latin, French

Venezuela

Area: 352,144 sq mi
(912,050 sq km)
Population: 31,800,000
Capital: Caracas, pop. 2,935,000
Currency: bolivar
Religion: Roman Catholic
Languages: Spanish, numerous indigenous dialects

Vietnam

Area: 127,844 sq mi
(331,114 sq km)
Population: 94,700,000
Capital: Hanoi, pop. 4,283,000
Currency: dong
Religions: Buddhist, Roman Catholic
Languages: Vietnamese, English, French, Chinese, Khmer

Yemen

Area: 207,286 sq mi
(536,869 sq km)
Population: 28,900,000
Capital: Sanaa, pop. 2,779,000
Currency: Yemeni rial
Religions: Muslim, including Shaf'i (Sunni)
and Zaydi (Shiite)
Language: Arabic

Zambia

Area: 290,586 sq mi
(752,614 sq km)
Population: 17,700,000
Capital: Lusaka, pop. 2,524,000
Currency: Zambian kwacha
Religions: Christian, Muslim, Hindu
Languages: English, Bemba, Kaonda, Lozi, Lunda, Luvale,
Nyanja, Tonga, about 70 other indigenous languages

Zimbabwe

Area: 150,872 sq mi
(390,757 sq km)
Population: 14,000,000
Capital: Harare, pop. 1,515,000
Currency: Zimbabwean dollar
Religions: Syncretic (part Christian, part indigenous
beliefs), Christian, indigenous beliefs
Languages: English, Shona, Sindebele, tribal dialects

THE POLITICAL UNITED STATES

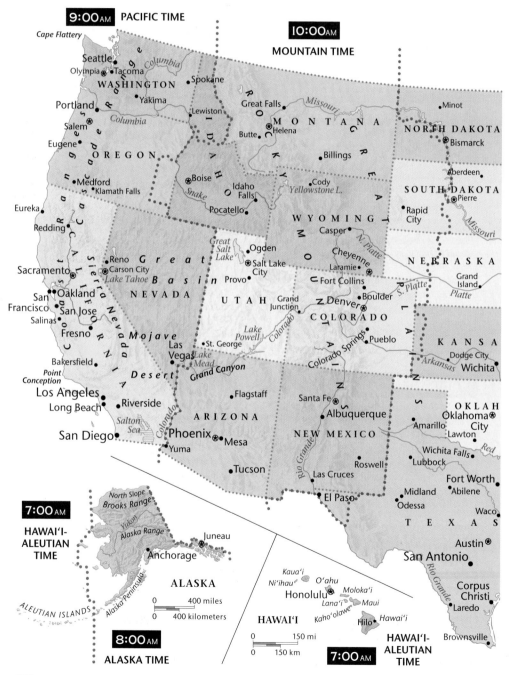

9:00AM **PACIFIC TIME**

10:00AM **MOUNTAIN TIME**

Cape Flattery

Seattle
Olympia • Tacoma
WASHINGTON • Spokane
Portland • Yakima
Columbia
Salem • Lewiston
Eugene • Columbia
OREGON

Great Falls
Missouri
M O N T A N A
Butte • Helena
Billings
Minot
NORTH DAKOTA
Bismarck
Aberdeen
SOUTH DAKOTA
Pierre

Medford • Boise
Klamath Falls • Snake Idaho Falls
Eureka • Pocatello
Redding

Yellowstone L.
Cody
W Y O M I N G
Casper
N. Platte
Rapid City
Missouri

Reno • G r e a t
Carson City
Lake Tahoe • B a s i n
Sacramento •
San • Oakland N E V A D A
Francisco • San Jose
Salinas •
Fresno •

Great Salt Lake
Ogden
Salt Lake City
Provo
U T A H Grand Junction

Cheyenne
Laramie
Fort Collins
Denver • Boulder
C O L O R A D O

N E B R A S K A
Grand Island
Platte
S. Platte

Bakersfield •
Point Conception
Los Angeles
Long Beach • Riverside
San Diego •

M o j a v e
Las Vegas • Lake Mead
D e s e r t
Grand Canyon
Salton Sea
Phoenix • • Mesa
Yuma

Lake Powell
St. George
Colorado
A R I Z O N A

Colorado Springs
Pueblo
K A N S A S
Dodge City
Arkansas
Wichita

Flagstaff
Santa Fe
Albuquerque
N E W M E X I C O
Las Cruces

Amarillo
O K L A H
Oklahoma City
Lawton
Wichita Falls
Red

Roswell
Lubbock
Fort Worth
Midland • Abilene
Odessa
Waco
T E X A S

El Paso
Rio Grande

7:00AM
HAWAI'I- ALEUTIAN TIME

North Slope
Brooks Range
Yukon
Alaska Range
Juneau
Anchorage
ALASKA
Alaska Peninsula
ALEUTIAN ISLANDS

0   400 miles
0   400 kilometers

Kaua'i
Ni'ihau • O'ahu
Honolulu • Moloka'i
Lana'i • Maui
HAWAI'I • Kaho'olawe • Hawai'i
Hilo

0   150 mi
0   150 km

Austin
San Antonio
Corpus Christi
Laredo
Brownsville

8:00AM
ALASKA TIME

7:00AM
HAWAI'I- ALEUTIAN TIME

The United States is made up of 50 states joined like a giant quilt. Each is unique, but together they make a national fabric held together by a constitution and a federal government. State boundaries, outlined in dotted lines on the map, set apart internal political units within the country. The national capital—Washington, D.C.—is marked by a star in a double circle. The capital of each state is marked by a star in a single circle.

11:00 AM
CENTRAL TIME

12:00 NOON
EASTERN TIME

0   300 miles
0   300 kilometers
Albers Conic Equal-Area Projection

TIME ZONES: Earth is divided into 24 time zones, each about 15 degrees of longitude wide, reflecting the distance Earth turns from west to east each hour. The U.S. is divided into six time zones, indicated by red dotted lines on the map.

319

THE PHYSICAL UNITED STATES

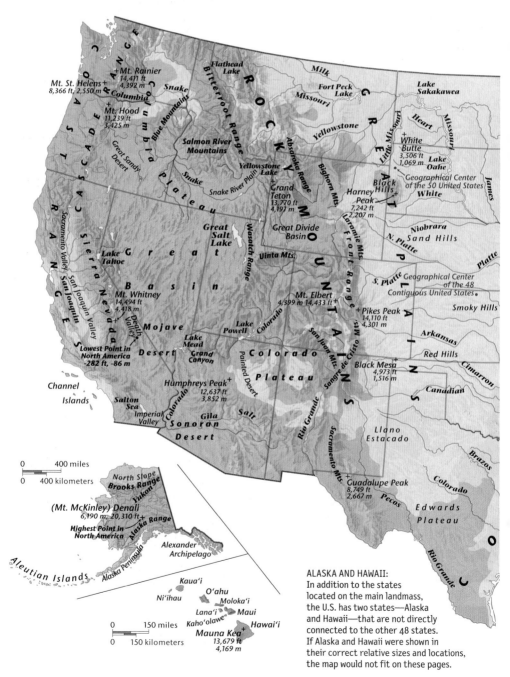

CASCADE RANGE

Mt. Rainier
14,411 ft
4,392 m

Mt. St. Helens
8,366 ft, 2,550 m

Columbia

Snake

Flathead
Lake

Bitterroot Range

ROCKY

Milk

Fort Peck
Lake

Missouri

Lake
Sakakawea

GREAT

Mt. Hood
11,239 ft
3,425 m

Blue Mountains

Great Sandy
Desert

Columbia Plateau

Salmon River
Mountains

Yellowstone

Yellowstone
Lake

Absaroka Range

Little Missouri

Missouri

Heart

White
Butte
3,506 ft
1,069 m

Lake
Oahe

Snake

Snake River Plain

Grand
Teton
13,770 ft
4,197 m

Bighorn Mts.

Black
Hills

Harney
Peak
7,242 ft
2,207 m

Geographical Center
of the 50 United States
White

James

Great
Salt
Lake

Wasatch Range

Great Divide
Basin

Uinta Mts.

Laramie Mts.

Front Range

MOUNTAINS

Niobrara

N. Platte

Sand Hills

Platte

Lake
Tahoe

Sierra Nevada

Great

Basin

S. Platte

Geographical Center
of the 48
Contiguous United States

Smoky Hills

Sacramento Valley

San Joaquin Valley

San Joaquin

Mt. Whitney
14,494 ft
4,418 m

Death Valley

Mojave

Mt. Elbert
4,399 m 14,433 ft

Pikes Peak
14,110 ft
4,301 m

San Juan Mts.

Colorado

Arkansas

Red Hills

Lake
Powell

Lake
Mead

Lowest Point in
North America
-282 ft, -86 m

Desert

Grand
Canyon

Colorado

Painted Desert

Colorado

Plateau

Sangre de Cristo Mts.

Black Mesa
4,973 ft
1,516 m

Cimarron

Channel
Islands

Humphreys Peak
12,637 ft
3,852 m

Salton
Sea

Imperial
Valley

Colorado

Gila

Sonoran

Desert

Salt

Rio Grande

Canadian

Llano
Estacado

Brazos

Sacramento Mts.

Guadalupe Peak
8,749 ft
2,667 m

Pecos

Colorado

Edwards
Plateau

Rio Grande

ALASKA AND HAWAII:

North Slope

Brooks Range

Yukon

(Mt. McKinley) Denali
6,190 m; 20,310 ft

Alaska Range

Highest Point in
North America

Aleutian Islands

Alaska Peninsula

Alexander
Archipelago

0   400 miles
0   400 kilometers

Kaua'i

Ni'ihau

O'ahu

Moloka'i

Lana'i   Maui

Kaho'olawe

Hawai'i

Mauna Kea
13,679 ft
4,169 m

0   150 miles
0   150 kilometers

In addition to the states
located on the main landmass,
the U.S. has two states—Alaska
and Hawaii—that are not directly
connected to the other 48 states.
If Alaska and Hawaii were shown in
their correct relative sizes and locations,
the map would not fit on these pages.

Stretching from the Atlantic Ocean in the east to the Pacific Ocean in the west, the United States is the third largest country (by area) in the world. Its physical diversity ranges from mountains to fertile plains and dry deserts. Shading on the map indicates changes in elevation, while colors show different vegetation patterns.

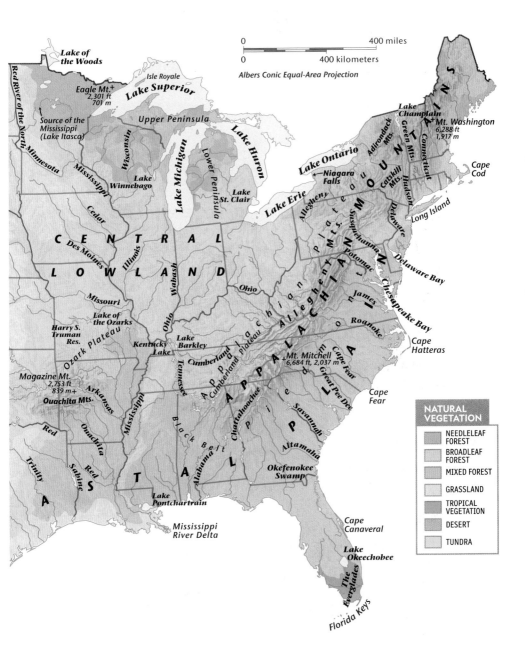

0   400 miles

0   400 kilometers

Albers Conic Equal-Area Projection

NATURAL VEGETATION

- NEEDLELEAF FOREST
- BROADLEAF FOREST
- MIXED FOREST
- GRASSLAND
- TROPICAL VEGETATION
- DESERT
- TUNDRA

THE STATES

From sea to shining sea, the United States of America is a nation of diversity. In the 244 years since its creation, the nation has grown to become home to a wide range of peoples, industries, and cultures. The following pages present a general overview of all 50 states in the U.S.

The country is generally divided into five large regions: the Northeast, the Southeast, the Midwest, the Southwest, and the West. Though loosely defined, these zones tend to share important similarities, including climate, history, and geography. The color key below provides a guide to which states are in each region.

The flags of each state and highlights of demography and industry are also included. These details offer a brief overview of each state.

In addition, each state's official flower and bird are identified.

Color Key by Region

Arizona

Area: 113,998 sq mi (295,256 sq km)
Population: 7,171,646
Capital: Phoenix, pop. 1,626,078
Largest city: Phoenix, pop. 1,626,078
Industry: Real estate, manufactured goods, retail, state and local government, transportation and public utilities, wholesale trade, health services
State flower/bird: Saguaro/cactus wren

> In Arizona, **CUTTING DOWN A SAGUARO CACTUS** could **RESULT** in **JAIL TIME.**

Arkansas

Area: 53,179 sq mi (137,732 sq km)
Population: 3,013,825
Capital: Little Rock, pop. 198,606
Largest city: Little Rock, pop. 198,606
Industry: Services, food processing, paper products, transportation, metal products, machinery, electronics
State flower/bird: Apple blossom/mockingbird

Alabama

Area: 52,419 sq mi (135,765 sq km)
Population: 4,887,871
Capital: Montgomery, pop. 199,518
Largest city: Birmingham, pop. 210,710
Industry: Retail and wholesale trade, services, government, finance, insurance, real estate, transportation, construction, communication
State flower/bird: Camellia/northern flicker

California

Area: 163,696 sq mi (423,972 sq km)
Population: 39,557,045
Capital: Sacramento, pop. 501,901
Largest city: Los Angeles, pop. 3,999,759
Industry: Electronic components and equipment, computers and computer software, tourism, food processing, entertainment, clothing
State flower/bird: Golden poppy/California quail

Alaska

Area: 663,267 sq mi (1,717,862 sq km)
Population: 737,438
Capital: Juneau, pop. 32,094
Largest city: Anchorage, pop. 294,356
Industry: Petroleum products, government, services, trade
State flower/bird: Forget-me-not/willow ptarmigan

Colorado

Area: 104,094 sq mi (269,602 sq km)
Population: 5,695,564
Capital: Denver, pop. 704,621
Largest city: Denver, pop. 704,621
Industry: Real estate, government, durable goods, communications, health and other services, nondurable goods, transportation
State flower/bird: Columbine/lark bunting

COLOR KEY ● Northeast ● Southeast

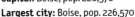

Connecticut

Area: 5,543 sq mi (14,357 sq km)
Population: 3,572,665
Capital: Hartford, pop. 123,400
Largest city: Bridgeport, pop. 146,579
Industry: Transportation equipment, metal products, machinery, electrical equipment, printing and publishing, scientific instruments, insurance
State flower/bird: Mountain laurel/robin

Delaware

Area: 2,489 sq mi (6,447 sq km)
Population: 967,171
Capital: Dover, pop. 37,538
Largest city: Wilmington, pop. 71,106
Industry: Food processing, chemicals, rubber and plastic products, scientific instruments, printing and publishing, financial services
State flower/bird: Peach blossom/blue hen chicken

Florida

Area: 65,755 sq mi (170,304 sq km)
Population: 21,299,325
Capital: Tallahassee, pop. 191,049
Largest city: Jacksonville, pop. 892,062
Industry: Tourism, health services, business services, communications, banking, electronic equipment, insurance
State flower/bird: Orange blossom/mockingbird

Georgia

Area: 59,425 sq mi (153,910 sq km)
Population: 10,519,475
Capital: Atlanta, pop. 486,290
Largest city: Atlanta, pop. 486,290
Industry: Textiles and clothing, transportation equipment, food processing, paper products, chemicals, electrical equipment, tourism
State flower/bird: Cherokee rose/brown thrasher

Hawaii

Area: 10,931 sq mi (28,311 sq km)
Population: 1,420,491
Capital: Honolulu, pop. 350,395
Largest city: Honolulu, pop. 350,395
Industry: Tourism, trade, finance, food processing, petroleum refining, stone, clay, glass products
State flower/bird: Hibiscus/Hawaiian goose (nene)

Idaho

Area: 83,570 sq mi (216,447 sq km)
Population: 1,754,208
Capital: Boise, pop. 226,570
Largest city: Boise, pop. 226,570
Industry: Electronics and computer equipment, tourism, food processing, forest products, mining
State flower/bird: Syringa (Lewis's mock orange)/ mountain bluebird

Illinois

Area: 57,914 sq mi (149,998 sq km)
Population: 12,741,080
Capital: Springfield, pop. 114,868
Largest city: Chicago, pop. 2,716,450
Industry: Industrial machinery, electronic equipment, food processing, chemicals, metals, printing and publishing, rubber and plastics, motor vehicles
State flower/bird: Violet/cardinal

Indiana

Area: 36,418 sq mi (94,322 sq km)
Population: 6,691,878
Capital: Indianapolis, pop. 863,002
Largest city: Indianapolis, pop. 863,002
Industry: Transportation equipment, steel, pharmaceutical and chemical products, machinery, petroleum, coal
State flower/bird: Peony/cardinal

Iowa

Area: 56,272 sq mi (145,743 sq km)
Population: 3,156,145
Capital: Des Moines, pop. 217,521
Largest city: Des Moines, pop. 217,521
Industry: Real estate, health services, industrial machinery, food processing, construction
State flower/bird: Wild rose/American goldfinch

An enormous **BALL OF POPCORN**— made from 900 pounds (408 kg) of popcorn—resides in **SAC CITY, IOWA.**

● Midwest   ● **Southwest**   ● West

Kansas

Area: 82,277 sq mi (213,097 sq km)
Population: 2,911,505
Capital: Topeka, pop. 126,587
Largest city: Wichita, pop. 390,591
Industry: Aircraft manufacturing, transportation equipment, construction, food processing, printing and publishing, health care
State flower/bird: Sunflower/western meadowlark

Kentucky

Area: 40,409 sq mi (104,659 sq km)
Population: 4,468,402
Capital: Frankfort, pop. 27,621
Largest city: Louisville, pop. 621,349
Industry: Manufacturing, services, government, finance, insurance, real estate, retail trade, transportation, wholesale trade, construction, mining
State flower/bird: Goldenrod/cardinal

Louisiana

Area: 51,840 sq mi (134,265 sq km)
Population: 4,659,978
Capital: Baton Rouge, pop. 225,374
Largest city: New Orleans, pop. 393,292
Industry: Chemicals, petroleum products, food processing, health services, tourism, oil and natural gas extraction, paper products
State flower/bird: Magnolia/brown pelican

PROFESSIONAL WRESTLING was once BANNED in LOUISIANA.

Maine

Area: 35,385 sq mi (91,646 sq km)
Population: 1,338,404
Capital: Augusta, pop. 18,594
Largest city: Portland, pop. 66,882
Industry: Health services, tourism, forest products, leather products, electrical equipment
State flower/bird: White pine cone and tassel/chickadee

Maryland

Area: 12,407 sq mi (32,133 sq km)
Population: 6,042,718
Capital: Annapolis, pop. 39,321
Largest city: Baltimore, pop. 611,648
Industry: Real estate, federal government, health services, business services, engineering services
State flower/bird: Black-eyed Susan/northern (Baltimore) oriole

Massachusetts

Area: 10,555 sq mi (27,336 sq km)
Population: 6,902,149
Capital: Boston, pop. 685,094
Largest city: Boston, pop. 685,094
Industry: Electrical equipment, machinery, metal products, scientific instruments, printing and publishing, tourism
State flower/bird: Mayflower/chickadee

Michigan

Area: 96,716 sq mi (250,495 sq km)
Population: 9,995,915
Capital: Lansing, pop. 116,986
Largest city: Detroit, pop. 673,104
Industry: Motor vehicles and parts, machinery, metal products, office furniture, tourism, chemicals
State flower/bird: Apple blossom/robin

Minnesota

Area: 86,939 sq mi (225,172 sq km)
Population: 5,611,179
Capital: St. Paul, pop. 306,621
Largest city: Minneapolis, pop. 422,331
Industry: Real estate, banking and insurance, industrial machinery, printing and publishing, food processing, scientific equipment
State flower/bird: Showy lady's slipper/common loon

Mississippi

Area: 48,430 sq mi (125,434 sq km)
Population: 2,986,530
Capital: Jackson, pop. 166,965
Largest city: Jackson, pop. 166,965
Industry: Petroleum products, health services, electronic equipment, transportation, banking, forest products, communications
State flower/bird: Magnolia/mockingbird

COLOR KEY ● Northeast ● Southeast

Missouri

Area: 69,704 sq mi (180,534 sq km)
Population: 6,126,452
Capital: Jefferson City, pop. 42,895
Largest city: Kansas City, pop. 488,943
Industry: Transportation equipment, food processing, chemicals, electrical equipment, metal products
State flower/bird: Hawthorn/eastern bluebird

Montana

Area: 147,042 sq mi (380,840 sq km)
Population: 1,062,305
Capital: Helena, pop. 31,429
Largest city: Billings, pop. 109,642
Industry: Forest products, food processing, mining, construction, tourism
State flower/bird: Bitterroot/western meadowlark

Nebraska

Area: 77,354 sq mi (200,346 sq km)
Population: 1,929,268
Capital: Lincoln, pop. 284,736
Largest city: Omaha, pop. 466,893
Industry: Food processing, machinery, electrical equipment, printing and publishing
State flower/bird: Goldenrod/western meadowlark

Nevada

Area: 110,561 sq mi (286,352 sq km)
Population: 3,034,392
Capital: Carson City, pop. 54,745
Largest city: Las Vegas, pop. 641,676
Industry: Tourism and gaming, mining, printing and publishing, food processing, electrical equipment
State flower/bird: Sagebrush/mountain bluebird

New Hampshire

Area: 9,350 sq mi (24,216 sq km)
Population: 1,356,458
Capital: Concord, pop. 43,019
Largest city: Manchester, pop. 111,196
Industry: Machinery, electronics, metal products
State flower/bird: Purple lilac/purple finch

New Jersey

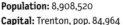

Area: 8,721 sq mi (22,588 sq km)
Population: 8,908,520
Capital: Trenton, pop. 84,964
Largest city: Newark, pop. 285,154
Industry: Machinery, electronics, metal products, chemicals
State flower/bird: Violet/American goldfinch

New Mexico

Area: 121,590 sq mi (314,917 sq km)
Population: 2,095,428
Capital: Santa Fe, pop. 83,776
Largest city: Albuquerque, pop. 558,545
Industry: Electronic equipment, state and local government, real estate, business services, federal government, oil and gas extraction, health services
State flower/bird: Yucca/roadrunner

New York

Area: 54,556 sq mi (141,300 sq km)
Population: 19,542,209
Capital: Albany, pop. 98,251
Largest city: New York City, pop. 8,622,698
Industry: Printing and publishing, machinery, computer products, finance, tourism
State flower/bird: Rose/eastern bluebird

Coyotes, skunks, deer, rabbits, opossum, and snapping turtles have all been spotted in NEW YORK CITY'S PARKS.

North Carolina

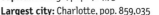

Area: 53,819 sq mi (139,390 sq km)
Population: 10,383,620
Capital: Raleigh, pop. 464,758
Largest city: Charlotte, pop. 859,035
Industry: Real estate, health services, chemicals, tobacco products, finance, textiles
State flower/bird: Flowering dogwood/cardinal

North Dakota

Area: 70,700 sq mi (183,113 sq km)
Population: 760,077
Capital: Bismarck, pop. 72,865
Largest city: Fargo, pop. 122,359
Industry: Services, government, finance, construction, transportation, oil and gas
State flower/bird: Wild prairie rose/ western meadowlark

Ohio

Area: 44,825 sq mi (116,097 sq km)
Population: 11,689,442
Capital: Columbus, pop. 879,170
Largest city: Columbus, pop. 879,170
Industry: Transportation equipment, metal products, machinery, food processing, electrical equipment
State flower/bird: Scarlet carnation/cardinal

Oklahoma

Area: 69,898 sq mi (181,036 sq km)
Population: 3,943,079
Capital: Oklahoma City, pop. 643,648
Largest city: Oklahoma City, pop. 643,648
Industry: Manufacturing, services, government, finance, insurance, real estate
State flower/bird: Mistletoe/scissor-tailed flycatcher

Oregon

Area: 98,381 sq mi (254,806 sq km)
Population: 4,190,713
Capital: Salem, pop. 169,798
Largest city: Portland, pop. 647,805
Industry: Real estate, retail and wholesale trade, electronic equipment, health services, construction, forest products, business services
State flower/bird: Oregon grape/western meadowlark

Pennsylvania

Area: 46,055 sq mi (119,283 sq km)
Population: 12,807,060
Capital: Harrisburg, pop. 49,192
Largest city: Philadelphia, pop. 1,580,863
Industry: Machinery, printing and publishing, forest products, metal products
State flower/bird: Mountain laurel/ruffed grouse

Rhode Island

Area: 1,545 sq mi (4,002 sq km)
Population: 1,057,315
Capital: Providence, pop. 180,393
Largest city: Providence, pop. 180,393
Industry: Health services, business services, silver and jewelry products, metal products
State flower/bird: Violet/Rhode Island red

South Carolina

Area: 32,020 sq mi (82,932 sq km)
Population: 5,084,127
Capital: Columbia, pop. 133,114
Largest city: Charleston, pop. 134,875
Industry: Service industries, tourism, chemicals, textiles, machinery, forest products
State flower/bird: Yellow jessamine/Carolina wren

3 cool things about SOUTH CAROLINA

1. The world's largest fire hydrant is in Columbia, South Carolina. The public work of art, known as Busted Plug, is as tall as a four-story building and is said to be sturdy enough to withstand a tornado.

2. The hottest pepper on the planet is grown on a farm on Fort Mill, South Carolina. The Carolina Reaper is said to be more than 200 times hotter than the spiciest jalapeño pepper.

3. South Carolina's Morgan Island is home to a population of some 3,500 Rhesus monkeys. Only researchers are allowed on the federally protected "Monkey Island," which is closed off to the general public.

South Dakota

Area: 77,117 sq mi (199,732 sq km)
Population: 882,235
Capital: Pierre, pop. 14,004
Largest city: Sioux Falls, pop. 176,888
Industry: Finance, services, manufacturing, government, retail trade, transportation and utilities, wholesale trade, construction, mining
State flower/bird: Pasqueflower/ring-necked pheasant

COLOR KEY ● Northeast ● Southeast

Tennessee

Area: 42,143 sq mi (109,151 sq km)
Population: 6,770,010
Capital: Nashville, pop. 667,560
Largest city: Nashville, pop. 667,560
Industry: Service industries, chemicals, transportation equipment, processed foods, machinery
State flower/bird: Iris/mockingbird

Texas

Area: 268,581 sq mi (695,624 sq km)
Population: 28,701,845
Capital: Austin, pop. 950,715
Largest city: Houston, pop. 2,312,717
Industry: Chemicals, machinery, electronics and computers, food products, petroleum and natural gas, transportation equipment
State flower/bird: Bluebonnet/mockingbird

Utah

Area: 84,899 sq mi (219,888 sq km)
Population: 3,161,105
Capital: Salt Lake City, pop. 200,544
Largest city: Salt Lake City, pop. 200,544
Industry: Government, manufacturing, real estate, construction, health services, business services, banking
State flower/bird: Sego lily/California gull

Vermont

Area: 9,614 sq mi (24,901 sq km)
Population: 626,299
Capital: Montpelier, pop. 7,484
Largest city: Burlington, pop. 42,239
Industry: Health services, tourism, finance, real estate, computer components, electrical parts, printing and publishing, machine tools
State flower/bird: Red clover/hermit thrush

Virginia

Area: 42,774 sq mi (110,785 sq km)
Population: 8,517,685
Capital: Richmond, pop. 227,032
Largest city: Virginia Beach, pop. 450,435
Industry: Food processing, communication and electronic equipment, transportation equipment, printing, shipbuilding, textiles
State flower/bird: Flowering dogwood/cardinal

Washington

Area: 71,300 sq mi (184,666 sq km)
Population: 7,535,591
Capital: Olympia, pop. 51,609
Largest city: Seattle, pop. 724,745
Industry: Aerospace, tourism, food processing, forest products, paper products, industrial machinery, printing and publishing, metals, computer software
State flower/bird: Coast rhododendron/Amer. goldfinch

> **WASHINGTON STATE FERRIES carry 22 million passengers per year—making them the WORLD'S MOST POPULAR ferry system.**

West Virginia

Area: 24,230 sq mi (62,755 sq km)
Population: 1,805,832
Capital: Charleston, pop. 47,929
Largest city: Charleston, pop. 47,929
Industry: Tourism, coal mining, chemicals, metal manufacturing, forest products, stone, clay, oil, glass products
State flower/bird: Rhododendron/cardinal

Wisconsin

Area: 65,498 sq mi (169,639 sq km)
Population: 5,813,568
Capital: Madison, pop. 255,214
Largest city: Milwaukee, pop. 595,351
Industry: Industrial machinery, paper products, food processing, metal products, electronic equipment, transportation
State flower/bird: Wood violet/robin

Wyoming

Area: 97,814 sq mi (253,337 sq km)
Population: 577,737
Capital: Cheyenne, pop. 63,624
Largest city: Cheyenne, pop. 63,624
Industry: Oil and natural gas, mining, generation of electricity, chemicals, tourism
State flower/bird: Indian paintbrush/western meadowlark

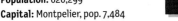

● Midwest ● **Southwest** ● West

THE TERRITORIES

The United States has 14 territories— political divisions that are not states. Three of these are in the Caribbean Sea, and the other 11 are in the Pacific Ocean.

St. John, U.S. Virgin Islands

Convention Center, San Juan, Puerto Rico

Talofofo Falls, Guam

U.S. CARIBBEAN TERRITORIES

Puerto Rico

Area: 3,508 sq mi (9,086 sq km)
Population: 3,337,177
Capital: San Juan, pop. 2,454,000
Languages: Spanish, English

U.S. Virgin Islands

Area: 149 sq mi (386 sq km)
Population: 106,977
Capital: Charlotte Amalie, pop. 52,000
Languages: English, Spanish or Spanish Creole, French or French Creole

U.S. PACIFIC TERRITORIES

American Samoa

Area: 77 sq mi (199 sq km)
Population: 50,826
Capital: Pago Pago, pop. 49,000
Language: Samoan

Guam

Area: 217 sq mi (561 sq km)
Population: 167,772
Capital: Hagåtña (Agana), pop. 147,000
Languages: English, Chamorro, Philippine languages

Northern Mariana Islands

Area: 184 sq mi (477 sq km)
Population: 51,994
Capital: Saipan, pop. 51,000
Languages: Philippine languages, Chinese, Chamorro, English

Other U.S. Territories

Baker Island, Howland Island, Jarvis Island, Johnston Atoll, Kingman Reef, Midway Islands, Palmyra Atoll, Wake Island, Navassa Island (in the Caribbean)

Figures for capital cities vary widely between sources because of differences in the way the area is defined and other projection methods.

THE U.S. CAPITAL

District of Columbia

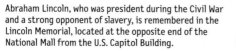

Area: 68 sq mi (177 sq km)
Population: 702,455

Abraham Lincoln, who was president during the Civil War and a strong opponent of slavery, is remembered in the Lincoln Memorial, located at the opposite end of the National Mall from the U.S. Capitol Building.

COLOR KEY ● Territories ● Northeast

BY THE NUMBERS!

RECORD SETTERS IN THE NATIONAL PARKS

Highest, longest, hottest, most visited: Our national parks are not only natural wonders—they're record setters! Check out the titles that these parks hold.

20,320 FEET (6,194 M)

THE FEAT: Highest Point in North America
THE PLACE: Denali National Park & Preserve (Mt. McKinley)

Rising from the Alaska Range, Denali is a block of granite that is half covered in permanent snowfields. Its name comes from the Athabaskan Indians and means "Great One."

134°F (57°C)

THE FEAT: Hottest Place on Earth
THE PLACE: Death Valley National Park

Death Valley holds the record for world's highest air temperature—recorded at Furnace Creek in 1913. It's also the lowest place in North America—the park's Badwater Basin is 282 feet (86 m) below sea level. The average annual rainfall in Death Valley, which is located in California and Nevada, is less than two inches (5 cm), making it the driest place in North America.

400 MILES (644 KM)

THE FEAT: Longest Known Cave System in the World
THE PLACE: Mammoth Cave system, Mammoth Cave National Park

Some 400 miles (644 km) of Kentucky's Mammoth Cave system have been explored, but no one really knows how far it extends, as new caverns continue to be discovered. Over 4,000 years ago, the first humans entered the cave, which contains more than 1,000 stalactite formations.

10,099,276 PEOPLE

THE FEAT: Most Visited National Park
THE PLACE: Great Smoky Mountains National Park

Attracting more than 10 million visitors per year, Great Smoky Mountains is the nation's busiest national park! Its central location in North Carolina and Tennessee is within a day or two's drive for two-thirds of the U.S. population. Famous for its diversity of plant and animal life, the park is home to some 65 species of mammals, more than 200 varieties of birds, 67 native fish species, and more than 80 types of reptiles and amphibians!

Wacky World ←

check out these **bizarre roadside attractions** from around the globe.

SHIN-YOKOHAMA RAMEN MUSEUM
Yokohama, Japan

Slurp up some fun at a museum dedicated to the beloved noodle dish. Popular in Japan for more than half a century, ramen today comes in different styles specific to the country's regions. Taste them all at the museum's nine restaurants, decide which you like best, and then purchase as many packets as you like to take home. In between bites, watch how the noodles are made, read about their history, and stroll sets made to mimic a 1950s Tokyo neighborhood.

Hop in your car and get out your camera—you'll definitely want some selfies with these strange sights. Found all over the globe, bizarre roadside attractions draw visitors who want to add a little wackiness to their vacations. Take a glimpse at five of the world's weirdest stop-and-stare spots.

Check out the book!

SUSPENDED WATER TAP
Ypres, Belgium

What's the trick to this floating faucet? A clear pipe inside the falling water creates the illusion. The supportive pipe carries water from a pool on the ground to the rear of the faucet. The water loops around and is spewed back out into the pool. That's why it looks like an unending flow of water. Now we're thirsty.

DRAGON BRIDGE
Da Nang, Vietnam

Drivers cruising through one Vietnamese metropolis can see a pretty epic sight: a mythical monster perched on one of the city's bridges. The six-lane crossing, which is the length of 55 school buses, was designed to resemble a dragon. (In Vietnamese culture, dragons symbolize good fortune.) The beastly bridge even "breathes" fire! A blowtorch-like device in the dragon's mouth can be timed to spew flames. This dragon-shaped bridge is really slaying it.

Over the years, Lucy has withstood fires, hurricanes, and raging parties in her belly.

LUCY THE ELEPHANT
Margate City, New Jersey, U.S.A.
No, you're not seeing things. That is a giant elephant on the horizon at the Jersey Shore. Her name is Lucy, and she's not your average pachyderm. All elephants are huge, but Lucy, made of wood and tin, stands 65 feet (19.8 m) high—taller than a six-story building. Built in 1881, Lucy has served as a jumbo-size billboard, a beach house, and a tavern. How do visitors get in? Her 22-foot (6.7-m)-tall legs hide spiral staircases that lead the way.

"Floating" faucets can also be found in Canada, England, Spain, Switzerland, and the United States.

The sculpture is as tall as some trees, but this tree won't be doing any growing.

TRAFFIC LIGHT TREE
London, England, U.K.
Money doesn't grow on trees—but traffic lights might! This 26-foot (8-m)-high treelike structure is made of 75 sets of traffic lights controlled by computers. The sculpture, created by a French artist to represent the energy of the city around it, has been a big hit with locals. Sounds like this fake tree has really taken root.

HOW TALL IS IT?

Burj Khalifa, located in Dubai in the United Arab Emirates, soars over half a mile (0.8 km) high. But how does that compare to other cool sights around the globe? Check out this lineup to find out!

The Willis Tower has **16,100** windows.

More than **36,000 stones** make up the Washington Monument.

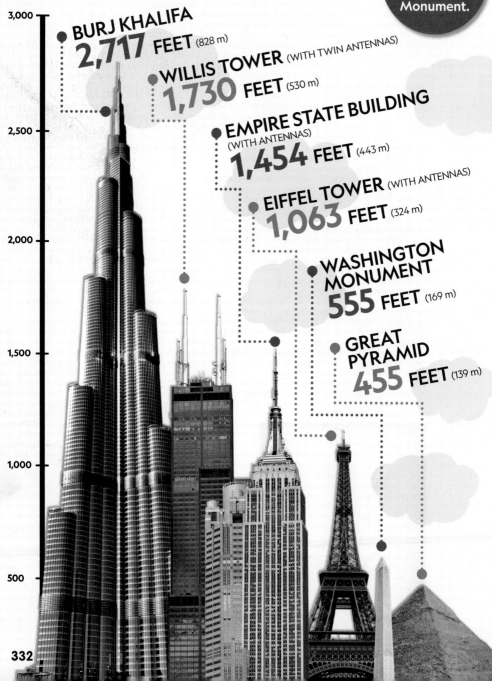

3,000

BURJ KHALIFA
2,717 FEET (828 m)

WILLIS TOWER (WITH TWIN ANTENNAS)
1,730 FEET (530 m)

2,500

EMPIRE STATE BUILDING
(WITH ANTENNAS)
1,454 FEET (443 m)

EIFFEL TOWER (WITH ANTENNAS)
1,063 FEET (324 m)

2,000

WASHINGTON MONUMENT
555 FEET (169 m)

1,500

GREAT PYRAMID
455 FEET (139 m)

1,000

500

NUMBER **CASCADE**

Victoria Falls, fed by the Zambezi River and located on the border of Zambia and Zimbabwe, is one of Africa's most famous and natural wonders and one of the most impressive waterfalls found on Earth. Explore some of the amazing stats behind this thunderous wall of water, which has shaped the land and ecosystem for millions of years.

142.7 BILLION GALLONS
(540 billion L)

of water drop over the falls per minute when the river is in full flood

354 FEET HIGH
(108 M)

5,538 FEET WIDE
(1,688 M)

1.25 MILES
(2 KM)
width of Zambezi River at the falls

0.3 MILE HIGH (0.5 KM)
maximum height of the spray plume

12 MILES (20 KM)
distance mist can be seen for

2,000,000 YEARS AGO
time when the falls started to form

3,000,000 YEARS OLD
age of stone artifacts made by early humans found near the falls

EXTREME
WEIRDNESS

VADER RULES THE SKY

WHAT León International Balloon Festival

WHERE León, Mexico

DETAILS This might be the Rebels' worst nightmare. Participants at this festival soared across the sky in giant hot-air balloons, such as this one shaped like Darth Vader's mask. More than a hundred balloons fly each year—anything from pandas to bees to scarecrows. But don't worry. This Vader's only full of hot air.

THE FORCE IS STRONG WITH THIS ONE.

DON'T MOW THIS GRASS.

WEAR YOUR LAWN

WHAT Grass-covered flip-flops

WHERE New South Wales Coast, Australia

DETAILS Want to feel the grass between your toes? Just plant your feet in these grass-topped flip-flops, designed to give you the sensation of being outdoors anytime. Don't worry about watering the sandals—the grass is actually a layer of artificial turf. You'll have some happy feet!

YOU'RE IN THE COLD SEAT.

ICE CUBE ON WHEELS

WHAT Truck made of ice

WHERE Hensall, Canada

DETAILS It's going to be an icy ride. This functional truck has a body made of 11,000 pounds (4,990 kg) of ice. Built over a base frame with wheels, the icy exterior covers a real engine, brakes, and steering wheel. It runs on a battery that's specially designed to start in frigid conditions that would keep most cars from revving up. The car can only go short distances—but what a great place to chill!

WILD VACATION

ENTER HERE!

SLEEP HERE!

Tree Hotel
NESTLING INTO NATURE

WHERE Dalat, Vietnam

HOW MUCH About $35 to $80 a night

WHY IT'S COOL One look at this hotel and you'll understand its nickname: "Crazy House." The bizarre lodging is designed to resemble a giant tree stump from the outside. The structure's cozy interior is filled with twisting passageways and 10 cavelike rooms, each with a different animal, insect, or plant theme. Visitors can unwind next to a fireplace shaped like a kangaroo or drift to sleep while staring at the stars through skylights in the Gourd Room. Guests can also wander through the garden, where eerie metal spiderwebs hang. More daring individuals can climb the winding walkways to the roof of the building and take in views of the surrounding city. From top to bottom, this hotel is insanely awesome.

COOL THINGS ABOUT VIETNAM

About 40 percent of the people in Vietnam have the last name Nguyen.

Grilled squid teeth are a popular snack in the country's coastal towns.

Vietnam is only 30 miles (48 km) wide at its narrowest point.

THINGS TO DO IN VIETNAM

Explore the bustling Cai Rang floating market, where boats are colorfully packed with fruits and vegetables for sale.

Sample traditional noodle soup called pho (pronounced FUH) from shops in Hanoi, the country's capital city.

Discover the palaces of former emperors inside the walls of the Hue Citadel, along the Perfume River.

QUIZ WHIZ

Is your geography
knowledge off the map?
Quiz yourself to find out!

Write your answers
on a piece of paper.
Then check them below.

1 Each year, monarch
butterflies migrate
from Mexico to _____.

a. Europe
b. Canada and the United States
c. Asia
d. Australia

2 A 5,500-year-old leather
_____ was once discovered
in an Armenian cave.

a. handbag
b. briefcase
c. shoe
d. wallet

3 The Traffic Light Tree is a
wacky roadside attraction
found in which city?

a. London, England
b. Chicago, Illinois
c. Prague, Czech Republic
d. Lima, Peru

4 **True or false?** An adult gentoo penguin makes
as many as 450 dives a day looking for food.

5 Which speedy animal
lives in Africa?

a. cheetah
b. antelope
c. wildebeest
d. all of the above

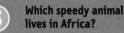

Not **STUMPED** yet? Check out the
NATIONAL GEOGRAPHIC KIDS QUIZ WHIZ collection
for more crazy **GEOGRAPHY** questions!

ANSWERS:
1. b; 2. c; 3. a; 4. True; 5. d

HOMEWORK HELP

Finding Your Way Around

Every map has a story to tell, but first you have to know how to read one. Maps represent information by using a language of symbols. Knowing how to read these symbols provides access to a wide range of information. Look at the scale and compass rose or arrow to understand distance and direction (see box below).

To find out what each symbol on a map means, you must use the key. It's your secret decoder—identifying information by each symbol on the map.

Latitude

Longitude

90°N (North Pole)
75°N
60°N
45°N
30°N
15°N
0° (Equator)
15°S
30°S
45°S

30°E
45°E
60°E
75°E
90°E
105°E
120°E
135°E

75°N
60°N
45°N
30°N
15°N
0° (Equator)
15°S
30°S
45°S

75°W
60°W
45°W
30°W
15°W
0° (Prime Meridian)
15°E
30°E
45°E
60°E
75°E

LATITUDE AND LONGITUDE

Latitude and longitude lines (above) help us determine locations on Earth. Every place on Earth has a special address called absolute location. Imaginary lines called lines of latitude run west to east, parallel to the Equator. These lines measure distance in degrees north or south from the Equator (0° latitude) to the North Pole (90° N) or to the South Pole (90° S). One degree of latitude is approximately 70 miles (113 km).

Lines of longitude run north to south, meeting at the poles. These lines measure distance in degrees east or west from 0° longitude (prime meridian) to 180° longitude. The prime meridian runs through Greenwich, England.

SCALE AND DIRECTION

The scale on a map can be shown as a fraction, as words, or as a line or bar. It relates distance on the map to distance in the real world. Sometimes the scale identifies the type of map projection. Maps may include an arrow or compass rose to indicate north on the map.

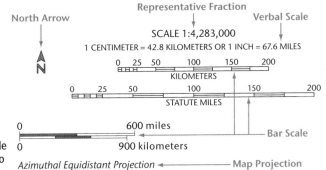

North Arrow

Representative Fraction

Verbal Scale

SCALE 1:4,283,000
1 CENTIMETER = 42.8 KILOMETERS OR 1 INCH = 67.6 MILES

N

0 25 50   100   150   200
KILOMETERS

0 25 50   100   150   200
STATUTE MILES

0   600 miles
0   900 kilometers

Bar Scale

Azimuthal Equidistant Projection ← Map Projection

GAME ANSWERS

What in the World?
page 164

Top row: mud, snowdrifts, lava
Middle row: moss, stones, palm leaf
Bottom row: tree trunk, iceberg, sand
             dunes

Find the Hidden Animals
page 165

1. E, 2. D, 3. A, 4. B, 5. F, 6. C

Signs of the Times
page 166
Signs 5 and 8 are fake.

Stump Your Parents
page 168

1. D, 2. B, 3. B, 4. C, 5. B, 6. C, 7. A,
8. A-5, B-4, C-2, D-3, E-1, 9. A, 10. B

What in the World?
page 170

Top row: balloon, swimming pool, dreidel
Middle row: clam, butterfly, macaw
Bottom row: stadium seats, sponge,
             toothbrush

Are You a Garbage Genius?
page 172
1. True, 2. True, 3. B, 4. C, 5. D

Find the Hidden Animals
page 173
1. B, 2. D, 3. E, 4. F, 5. A, 6. C

Stump Your Parents
page 175
1. C, 2. C, 3. D, 4. A, 5. B, 6. A, 7. D,
8. C, 9. C, 10. B

Movie Madness
page 176

What in the World?
page 178

Top row: galaxy, astronaut, moon
Middle row: space shuttle, sun, comet
Bottom row: Saturn, Mars rover,
             satellite

Want to Learn More?

Find more information about topics in this book in these National Geographic Kids resources.

Absolute Expert series

Weird But True series

Just Joking series

5,000 Awesome Facts (About Everything!) series

The Ultimate Book of Sharks
Brian Skerry
May 2018

Animal Smackdown
Emily Krieger
August 2018

Why Not?: Over 1,111 Answers to Everything
Crispin Boyer
August 2018

Dog Science Unleashed
Jodi Wheeler-Toppen
August 2018

How Things Work: Then and Now
T. J. Resler
October 2018

1,000 Facts About Ancient Egypt
Nancy Honovich
February 2019

Funny Animals
April 2019

125 True Stories of Amazing Animal Friendships
May 2018

Extreme Records
Julie Beer and Michelle Harris
June 2018

Animal Zombies!
Chana Stiefel
August 2018

Food Fight!
Tanya Steel
September 2018

Ultimate Predatorpedia
Christina Wilsdon
October 2018

Abbreviations:
AL: Alamy Stock Photo
DRMS: Dreamstime
GI: Getty Images
IS: iStockphoto
MP: Minden Pictures
NGIC: National Geographic Image Collection
SS: Shutterstock

All Maps
By National Geographic unless otherwise noted

All Illustrations & Charts
By Stuart Armstrong unless otherwise noted

Front Cover
(bear), Donald M. Jones/MP; (macaw), Rinus Baak/DRMS; (hoverboard), Zinkevych/GI

Spine
Donald M. Jones/MP

Back Cover
(Earth), Alex Staroseltsev/SS; (robot), julos/IS/GI; (dolphin), Donhype/IS; (spinning Earth), Johan Swanepoel/SS; (VR goggles), izusek/GI; (Roman Colosseum), Marco Rubino/SS; (red-eyed tree frog), Photolukacs/SS

Front Matter (2–7)
2-3, Katherine Feng/MP; 5 (UP LE), Image Source RF/Justin Lewis/GI; 5 (UP CTR LE), Sean Crane/MP; 5 (UP CTR RT), e-volo/Cover Images/Newscom; 5 (LO LE), Stefano Boeri Archietti; 5 (LO RT), Rebecca Hale/NG Staff; 6 (UP LE), Douglas Peebles/GI; 6 (UP RT), Zee/AL; 6 (UP CTR LE), SpaceX/GI; 6 (UP CTR RT), Don Smith/GI; 6 (LO CTR LE), Anup Shah/MP; 6 (LO CTR RT), Dan Sipple; 6 (LO LE), Pat Morrow/NGIC; 6 (LO RT), Brian J. Skerry/NGIC; 7 (UP LE), Room RF/GI; 7 (UP RT), Mike Hill/GI; 7 (CTR LE), IS/GI; 7 (LO LE), MelindaChan/GI

Your World 2020 (8–17)
8-9, Image Source/GI; 10 (UP LE), Katherine Feng/MP; 10 (UP RT), Bill Ingalls/NASA; 10 (LO LE), Reinhard Dirscherl/ullstein bild/GI; 10 (LO RT), R.M. Nunes/SS; 11 (UP LE), Joel_420/SS; 11 (UP RT), Lori Epstein/NG Staff; 11 (CTR LE), PictureLux/The Hollywood Archive/AL; 11 (CTR RT), Tui De Roy/MP; 11 (LO LE), Mark Agnor/SS; 11 (LO CTR), Mark Agnor/SS; 11 (LO RT), pictoKraft/AL; 12 (UP), Peter Jolly Northpix; 12 (LO LE), Omar Marques/Anadolu Agency/GI; 12 (LO RT), Piotr Nowak/AFP/GI; 13 (UP), The Asahi Shimbun/GI; 13 (CTR CTR), Tony Duffy/GI Sport/GI; 13 (CTR RT), Steve Russell/Toronto Star/GI; 13 (LO LE), Kyodo News Stills/GI; 13 (LO RT), Mark Ralston/AFP/GI; 14 (UP & CTR), ©2016 BRAVE ROBOTICS Inc., Asratec Corp./J-deite Ride JH-001Project; 14 (LO), Susan Schmitz/SS; 15 (UP), Tom Hartman/Dearhearts Wildlife Photography; 15 (LO), Anthony Quintano; 16 (UP CTR), Johnfoto/DRMS; 16 (UP LE), Tim Pelling/First Light/GI; 16 (UP RT), Simon Balson/AL; 16 (CTR LE), Kurit afshen/SS; 16 (CTR RT), Tracy Whiteside/SS; 16 (LO CTR LE), Shane Myers Photography/SS; 16 (LO CTR RT), Joseph Sohm/SS; 16 (LO LE), amenic181/SS; 16 (LO RT), GeniusKp/SS; 17 (UP), Louis B. Ruediger/Pittsburgh

Tribune-Review/AP Photo; 17 (CTR), Roland Weihrauch/picture-alliance/dpa/AP Photo; 17 (LO), Utelias Technologies Oy (Curious Technologies Ltd)

Amazing Animals (18–73)
18-19, Sean Crane/MP; 20 (LE), Felis Images-Robin Darius Conz; 20 (RT), Shekar Dattatri/NGIC; 21 (UP), Tdee Photo-cm/SS; 21 (LO), Colette3/SS; 22 (UP & CTR), Shelly Roche; 22 (LO), AP Photo/Frogwatch, HO; 23 (UP), Kaïl Marie, Director/CEO; 23 (LO), Karine Aigner/NG Staff; 24 (both), Rebecca Grunwell/The Gisborne Herald; 25 (both), Conny Schmidt/Caters News Agency; 26 (UP), buteo/SS; 26 (CTR), DioGen/SS; 26 (LO), Nick Garbutt; 27 (UP LE), Kant Liang/EyeEm/GI; 27 (UP RT), reptiles-4all/SS; 27 (CTR LE), Hiroya Minakuchi/MP; 27 (CTR RT), FP media/SS; 27 (LO), Aleksandar Dickov/SS; 28 (UP), Photoshot License Ltd/AL; 28 (LO), Steve Winter/NGIC; 29 (LE), Tom Brakefield/Corbis/GI; 29 (RT), James Kaiser; 30 (UP), Stephen Belcher/MP; 30 (LO), Royal Veterinary College, University of London; 31, Chris Johns/NG Staff; 32 (UP), Klein and Hubert/MP; 32 (LO LE), Stephen Dalton/MP; 32 (LO RT), Christian Ziegler/MP; 33 (UP RT), Paul Souders/GI; 33 (LO LE), Juan Carlos Muñoz/GI; 33 (all others), Ingo Arndt/MP; 34 (UP), Paul Souders/GI; 34 (CTR LE), EcoPrint/SS; 34 (LO RT), Age Fotostock/SuperStock; 34 (LO RT), Beverly Joubert/NGIC; 35 (UP), Andy Rouse/Stone/GI; 35 (LO), Albert Froneman; 36 (LO LE), Maria Diekmann/REST; 36 (LO LE inset), Jamie Trueblood/Columbia Pictures/Courtesy Everett Collection; 36 (LO RT), Suzi Eszterhas/MP; 36 (LO RT inset), 20th Century Fox/Entertainment Pictures/ZUMAPRESS; 37 (UP), Christian Boix/Africa Geographic; 37 (LO CTR LE), imageBROKER/AL; 37 (UP CTR LE & UP CTR RT), J Dennis Nigel/GI; 37 (LO CTR), Walt Disney Studios Motion Pictures/Courtesy Everett Collection; 37 (LO CTR RT), Marvel Studios/Collection Christophel/AL; 38-39 (background), Flip Nicklin/MP; 38 (LO), Brandon Cole/AL; 39 (LE), Doug Perrine/Seapics.com; 39 (RT), Tom & Pat Leeson/Ardea; 40 (UP LE), Donald M Jones/MP; 40 (UP RT), Milo Burcham/Design Pics INC/AL; 40 (LO LE), Doc White/Nature Picture Library; 40 (LO RT), Enrique R Aguirre Aves/GI; 41 (UP), John C. Lewis/SeaPics.com; 41 (CTR LE & CTR RT), Gary Bell/oceanwideimages.com; 41 (LO LE), Jeff Rotman/SeaPics.com; 41 (LO RT), Doug Perrine/SeaPics.com; 42 (UP), Norbert Wu/MP; 42 (LO), Claudio Contreres/NPL/MP; 43 (UP & LO RT), Doug Perrine/naturepl.com; 43 (CTR RT), SA Team/Foto Nature/MP; 43 (CTR LE), Claudio Contreras/Nature Picture Library; 44 (UP), Kevin Elsby/AL; 44 (CTR), Solent News and Photos; 44 (LO LE), Steve Parish; 44-45 (LO), Photo by Newspix/Rex USA; 45 (UP), Lynn M. Stone/Nature Picture Library; 45 (CTR), Reuters/ChinaDaily; 46 (UP LE), Mark Carwardine/ARDEA; 46 (UP RT & LO), Steven J. Kazlowski/AL; 47 (all), Adrian Bailey; 48 (UP RT), Cosmin Manci/SS; 48 (UP CTR LE), Ingo Arndt/naturepl.com; 48 (UP CTR RT), Dr. James L. Castner/Visuals Unlimited, Inc.; 48 (LO CTR LE), Alex Hyde/naturepl.com; 48 (LO LE), NHPA/SuperStock; 48 (LO RT), Chris

Mattison/FLPA/MP; 49 (UP LE), Alex Hyde/NaturePL.com/GI; 49 (UP RT), PREMAPHOTOS/naturepl.com; 49 (CTR LE), Christopher Smith/AL; 49 (CTR RT), Kazuo Unno/Nature Production/MP; 49 (LO), NH/SS; 50 (UP LE), Brian Kenney; 50 (UP RT), Art Wolfe/Stone/GI; 50 (LO), Ingo Arndt/MP; 51, Vicki Beaver/AL; 52 (CTR), James L. Stanfield/NGIC; 52 (LO RT), AP Images/Wide World Photos; 53 (UP), David Martinez; 53 (LO), Tom Kochel; 54-55 (both), Matthew Rakola; 56 (UP), AnetaPics/SS; 56 (LO), Suzi Eszterhas/MP; 57 (LO LE), Gerard Lacz/PhotoLibrary/GI; 57 (LO RT), ZSSD/MP; 57 (UP), Shin Yoshino/MP; 58 (UP LE), Eastcott Momatiuk/GI; 58 (LO LE), Gerry Ellis/Digital Vision; 58 (RT), Suzi Eszterhas/MP; 59 (UP), Jim Zuckerman/Kimball Stock; 59 (LO), Cincinnati Zoo; 60, Marion Vollborn/BIA/MP; 61 (UP LE), Suzi Eszterhas/MP; 61 (UP RT), Thomas Mangelsen/MP; 61 (LO LE), Grambo/GI; 61 (LO RT), Bengt Lundberg/naturepl.com; 62 (UP LE), Cabrillo Marine Aquarium/Caters News; 62 (UP RT), Karl Ammann/npl/MP; 62 (LO), Tui De Roy/MP; 63 (UP), Donald M. Jones/MP; 63 (LO), Ingo Arndt/Nature Picture Library; 64 (UP), Chris Butler/Science Photo Library/Photo Researchers, Inc.; 64 (CTR), Publiphoto/Photo Researchers, Inc.; 64 (LO), Pixeldust Studios/NGIC; 65 (A, D), Publiphoto/Photo Researchers, Inc.; 65 (B), Laurie O'Keefe/Photo Researchers, Inc.; 65 (C), Chris Butler/Photo Researchers, Inc.; 65 (E), image courtesy of Project Exploration; 66 (both), Andrea Meyer/SS; 67 (UP LE), Photo courtesy of the Royal Tyrrell Museum of Palaeontology, Drumheller, Alberta; 67 (UP RT), Andrew McAfee, Carnegie Museum of Natural History; 67 (LO), Peter Trusler; 68 (both), Franco Tempesta; 69 (UP), Catmando/SS; 69 (CTR), Franco Tempesta; 69 (LO), Leonello Calvetti/SS; 70 (UP & CTR), Franco Tempesta; 70 (LO), Photo by Roderick Mickens, American Museum of Natural History; 71 (LO LE), Julius Csotonyi; 71 (all others), Franco Tempesta; 72 (UP RT), Milo Burcham/Design Pics INC/AL; 72 (UP LE), Christian Ziegler/MP; 72 (CTR RT), Lionello Calvetti/SS; 72 (LO RT), Kant Liang/EyeEm/GI/GI; 73, GOLFX/SS

Science and Technology (74–99)
74-75, e-volo/Cover Images/Newscom; 76 (UP), Kakani Katija; 76 (inset), Todd Walsh/MBARI; 77 (UP), Peter Bennett/Universal Images Group Editorial/GI; 77 (CTR), Kim Reisenbichler/MBARI; 77 (LO), Kakani Katija; 78 (UP & UP CTR), VINCENT CALLEBAUT ARCHITECTURES, PARIS; 78 (LO CTR RT & LO RT), Foldimate; 78 (LO LE UP), Hammacher Schlemmer; 78 (LO LE LO), tassel78/SS; 79 (UP LE & UP CTR), PancakeBot; 79 (UP RT & CTR RT), Oombrella; 79 (LO CTR RT), Airbus; 79 (LO), Martin Heltai of Perlan Project; 80-83, Mondolithic Studios; 84, Ted Kinsman/Science Source; 85 (A), Sebastian Kaulitzki/SS; 85 (B), Steve Gschmeissner/Photo Researchers, Inc.; 85 (C), Volker Steger/Christian Bardele/Photo Researchers, Inc.; 85 (LO CTR LE), ancelpics/SS; 85 (LO CTR RT), sgame/SS; 85 (LO LE), puwanai/SS; 85 (LO RT),

kwest/SS; 86 (UP), FotograFFF/SS; 86 (LO), Craig Tuttle/Corbis/GI; 87 (UP), Lori Epstein/NG Staff; 87 (LO LE), Lori Epstein/NG Staff; 87 (LO RT), Science Picture Co/Collection Mix: Subjects RM/GI; 87 (CTR), Lori Epstein/NG Staff; 88-89, Simon Fraser/Science Source; 90 (UP), Roger Harris/Science Source; 90 (LO), Shaber/SS; 91, Tim Vernon/SPL/Science Source; 92 (UP), Cynthia Turner; 92 (LO), cobalt88/SS; 93 (CTR), Heritage Image Partnership Ltd/AL; 93 (LO), bgblue/IS/GI; 94 (UP LE), Dimarion/SS; 94 (UP RT), Eraxion/IS; 94 (CTR LE), Microfield Scientific Ltd./Science Source; 94 (CTR), mrfiza/SS; 94 (LO), iLexx/IS; 95 (UP), Jani Bryson/IS; 95 (CTR), MyImages - Micha/SS; 95 (LO), RapidEye/IS; 96-97 (all), Matthew Rakola; 98 (UP), FotograFFF/SS; 98 (CTR RT), Ted Kinsman/Science Source; 98 (LO LE), VINCENT CALLEBAUT ARCHITECTURES, PARIS; 99, Klaus Vedfelt/GI

Going Green (100–115)

100-101, Stefano Boeri Architetti; 102 (UP), Gemma Atwal; 102 (inset), Peter Anthony; 103 (UP), Streliuk Aleksei/DRMS; 103 (LO), Todd Paris/UAF; 104-105 (background), Wildlife in Crisis; 104 (UP), Wildlife in Crisis; 105 (UP & CTR LE), Marie De Stefanis/The Marine Mammal Center; 105 (CTR RT & LO), Wildlife in Crisis; 106 (UP), Scanrail/DRMS; 106 (CTR), Sean Pavone/DRMS; 106 (LO), Rodrigo Kristensen/SS; 107 (background), Caters News Agency; 107 (CTR RT), Jamie Squire/GI; 107 (CTR), Joao Sabino/Solent News/REX/SS; 107 (LO RT), Courtesy of Austin-Mergold; 107 (LO LE), Dirty Sugar Photography; 108, CnOra/GI; 109 (UP), Rich Carey/SS; 109 (LO), Jimmy Cumming/GI; 111 (UP), James Stone/Chasing Light Photography/GI; 111 (LO), James Balog/NGIC; 112 (CTR), Rebecca Hale/NG Staff; 112 (photo collage—redwood), FogStock LLC/Index Stock; 112 (photo collage—cat), Digital Vision/Punchstock; 112 (photo collage—ball), Royalty-Free/Corbis; 112 (photo collage—ice cream), Photodisc Green/GI; 112 (photo collage—dog), Royalty-Free/Corbis; 112 (photo collage—fire hydrant), Burke/Triolo/Brand X Pictures/Jupiter Images; 112 (photo collage—genie lamp), Burke/Triolo/Brand X Pictures/Jupiter Images; 112 (photo collage—girl), Rubberball Productions/GI; 112 (photo collage—WHOA sign), Thinkstock/Jupiter Images; 113, Rebecca Hale/NG Staff; 114 (UP), Scanrail/DRMS; 114 (CTR), Jim Cumming/GI; 114 (LO), Rich Carey/SS

Culture Connection (116–139)

116-117, Douglas Peebles/GI; 118 (UP), Nick Kato; 118 (inset), Kauila Barber; 119 (UP), Nick Kato; 119 (LO), Elizabeth Lindsey; 120-121 (UP), fotohunter/SS; 120 (UP LE), CreativeNature.nl/SS; 120 (UP RT), pat-tarastock/SS; 120 (LO LE), Tubol Evgeniya/SS; 120 (LO), imageBROKER/AL; 121 (UP), Jeremy Villasis/Demotix/Corbis; 121 (CTR), Zee/AL; 121 (LO), wacpan/SS; 122 (UP), Ajay Verma/Reuters; 122 (LO), Rubens Chaves/Tips Italia/Photolibrary; 123, Chonnanit/SS; 124 (UP LE), Splash News/NewsCom; 124 (LO RT), Fuse/GI; 124 (LO LE), Timothy A. Clary/

AFP/GI; 124 (LO RT), Timothy A. Clary/AFP/GI; 125-127 (all), Rebecca Hale/NG Staff; 128 (UP LE), Ivan Vdovin/AL; 128 (UP CTR), maogg/GI; 128 (UP RT), Paul Poplis/GI; 128 (CTR LE), Mlenny/IS; 128 (CTR RT), Jack Guez/AFP/GI; 128 (LO LE), Courtesy of The Banknote Book; 128 (LO RT), Ninette Maumus/AL; 129 (UP LE), Numismatic Guaranty Corporation (NGC); 129 (UP RT), Comstock/GI; 129 (UP CTR LE), Igor Stramyk/SS; 129 (LO CTR LE), Splash News/Newscom; 129 (LO CTR RT), D. Hurst/AL; 129 (LO CTR RT), "MoneyDress" with "Colonial Dress" behind. Paper currency and frame, Lifesize © Susan Stockwell 2010. © photo Colin Hampden-White 2010; 129 (LO RT), Kelley Miller/NG Staff; 130, Mark Thiessen/NG Staff; 131 (both), Mark Thiessen/NG Staff; 133, fcknimages/GI; 134 (LE), John Hazard; 134 (RT), Jose Ignacio Soto/SS; 135 (LE), Corey Ford/DRMS; 135 (RT), Photosani/SS; 136 (UP), Randy Olson; 136 (LO LE), Martin Gray/NGIC; 136 (LO RT), Sam Panthaky/AFP/GI; 137 (UP), Filippo Monteforte/GI; 137 (LO LE), Reza/NGIC; 137 (LO RT), Richard Nowitz/NGIC; 138 (UP), fcknimages/IS/GI; 138 (LO LE), "MoneyDress" with "Colonial Dress" behind. Paper currency and frame, Lifesize © Susan Stockwell 2010. © photo Colin Hampden-White 2010; 138 (LO RT), Mark Thiessen/NG Staff; 139 (UP LE), spatuletail/SS; 139 (UP RT), PictureLake/GI; 139 (CTR), cifotart/SS; 139 (LO), zydesign/SS

Space and Earth (140–161)

140-141, SpaceX/GI; 142 (UP), Kim Huppert; 142 (inset), Jordan Krcmaric; 143 (UP), Rafal Cichawa/SS; 143 (CTR & LO), Christine Y. Chen; 144-145 (CTR), Mark Garlick/Science Photo Library; 144 (LO), NASA/CXC/IOA/A FABIAN ETAL/Science Photo Library; 145 (UP), NASA, ESA and M.J. Jee (Johns Hopkins University); 145 (LO), M. Markevitch/CXC/CFA/NASA/Science Photo Library; 146-147, David Aguilar; 148 (UP), David Aguilar; 149 (all), Mondolithic Studios; 150 (background UP), Alexxandar/GI; 150 (UP RT), Walter Myers/Stocktrek Images/Corbis/GI; 150 (CTR RT), Tony & Daphne Hallas/Photo Researchers, Inc.; 150 (LO RT), Don Smith/GI; 151 (UP), NASA/Science Faction/SuperStock; 151 (LO), NASA; 152 (UP), Ralph Lee Hopkins/NGIC; 152 (UP LE and RT), Visuals Unlimited/GI; 152 (CTR LE), Visuals Unlimited/Corbis; 152 (CTR RT), Dirk Wiersma/Photo Researchers, Inc.; 152 (LO LE), Charles D. Winters/Photo Researchers, Inc.; 152 (LO RT), Theodore Clutter/Photo Researchers, Inc.; 153 (UP), NGIC; 154 (UP LE), Panoramic Stock Images/NGIC; 154 (UP RT), Charles D. Winters/Photo Researchers, Inc.; 154 (CTR), Ted Clutter/Photo Researchers, Inc.; 154 (LO LE), Jim Lopes/SS; 154 (LO RT), Jim Richardson/NGIC; 155 (UP LE), Scenics & Science/AL; 155 (UP RT), Mark A. Shneider/Photo Researchers, Inc.; 155 (UP CTR LE), Ken Lucas/Visuals Unlimited; 155 (UP CTR RT), Carsten Peter/NGIC; 155 (LO CTR), Dirk Wiersma/Photo Researchers, Inc.; 155 (LO CTR RT), Arturo Limon/SS; 155 (LO RT), Goran Bogicevic/SS; 156, Illustration by Frank Ippolito; 157 (UP LE), All Canada Photos/AL; 157 (UP RT), Salvatore Gebbia/National

Geographic My Shot; 157 (CTR LE), NASA; 157 (CTR RT), Diane Cook & Len Jenshel/NGIC; 157 (LO LE), Image Science and Analysis Laboratory, NASA-Johnson Space Center. "The Gateway to Astronaut Photography of Earth."; 157 (LO RT), Douglas Peebles Photography/AL; 158-159 (all), Denis Budkov/Caters News; 160 (UP), Don Smith/GI; 160 (CTR), All Canada Photos/AL; 160 (LO), Visuals Unlimited/Corbis; 161, pixhook/IS

Fun and Games (162–181)

162-163, Anup Shah/MP; 164 (UP LE), Punchstock; 164 (UP CTR), Photodisc Blue/GI; 164 (UP RT), PictureQuest; 164 (CTR LE), Pal Hermansen/GI; 164 (CTR), Punchstock; 164 (CTR RT), Vibe Images/SS; 164 (LO LE), Anthony Ise/GI; 164 (LO CTR), Punchstock; 164 (LO RT), Denis Burdin/SS; 165 (UP LE), EEI_Tony/GI; 165 (UP RT), Joel Sartore/NGIC; 165 (CTR LE), Tui De Roy/MP; 165 (CTR RT), Jack Goldfarb/Design Pics/Corbis/GI; 165 (LO LE), Fabio Liverani/NPL/MP; 165 (LO RT), Exactostock/SuperStock; 166 (#1), Charles Gullung/GI; 166 (#2), Photo Resource Hawaii/AL; 166 (#3), Slim Aarons/Hulton Archive/GI; 166 (#4), Joseph Sohm/Visions of America/Corbis; 166 (#5), Thinkstock Images/Jupiter Images; 166 (#6), Owaki/Kulla/GI; 166 (#7), Jack Sullivan/AL; 166 (#8), Dale O'Dell 2008; 166 (#9), Jeff Greenberg/UIG/GI; 167, Dan Sipple; 168 (UP LE), Sergey Alimov/GI; 168 (UP RT), Sorin Rechitan/EyeEm/GI; 168 (CTR RT), NASA/Paolo Nespoli; 168 (UP RT), Globe Photos/ZUMAPRESS; 168 (LO LE), Michael and Patricia Fogden/MP; 169, Chris Ware; 170 (UP LE), artpartner-images.com/AL; 170 (UP LE), napocska/SS; 170 (UP RT), PNC/Photodisc/GI; 170 (CTR LE), Khoroshunova Olga/SS; 170 (CTR), Dobermaraner/SS; 170 (CTR RT), Ian Duffield/SS; 170 (LO CTR), Medioimages/Jupiterimages; 170 (LO CTR), LWA/Photodisc/GI; Esa Hiltula/AL; 171 (UP), Kitchin & Hurst/leesonphoto; 171 (CTR), Elvele Images Ltd/AL; 171 (CTR), Pioneer111/DRMS; 171 (LO LE), Fuse/GI; 171 (LO RT), RubberBall/SuperStock; 172 (UP CTR), Rita Kochmarjova/SS; 172 (UP RT), Autthaphol Khoonpijit/DRMS; 172 (UP CTR RT), Nerthuz/SS; 172 (UP CTR), Mdorottya/DRMS; 172 (CTR), Skypixel/DRMS; 172 (LO CTR RT), Melinda Fawver/SS; 172 (LO LE), Domiciano Pablo Romero Franco/DRMS; 172 (LO CTR), Martinmark/DRMS; 173 (UP), Robert Fowler/SS; 173 (CTR LE), Valerie Taylor/Ardea; 173 (UP CTR RT), DARIYASINGH/IS/GI; 173 (LO LE), Iren Silence/SS; 173 (LO CTR RT), Don Johnston/GI; 173 (LO RT), Rafael Martos Martins/SS; 174, Dan Sipple; 175 (UP LE), Rinus Baak/DRMS; 175 (UP RT), Richard Susanto/SS; 175 (CTR LE), weerapong worranam/SS; 175 (CTR RT), M. Unal Ozmen/SS; 175 (LO LE), Dobermaraner/SS; 175 (LO RT), somchaij/SS; 176, MIGY; 177 (UP RT), Tim Laman/NGIC; 177 (A), Stephen St. John/NGIC; 177 (B), Joel Sartore/NGIC; 177 (C), Robert Harding/NGIC; 177 (UP RT INSET), Uwe Bergwitz/SS; 177 (UP CTR RT), Ellen Goff/Danita Delimont/SS; 177 (CTR LE), Westend61 Premium/SS; 177 (CTR RT), Westend61 Premium/SS; 177 (LO CTR RT), Michael Durham/MP; 178 (UP LE), David Herraez

Calzada/SS; 178 (UP CTR), Andrey Armyagov/SS; 178 (UP RT), Kei Shooting/SS; 178 (CTR LE), Mikephotos/DRMS; 178 (CTR), NASA/SDO; 178 (CTR RT), NASA/MSFC/MEO/AAron Kingery; 178 (LO LE), MarcelClemens/SS; 178 (LO CTR), NASA; 178 (LO RT), Andrey Armyagov/SS; 179, Dan Sipple; 180-181, Strika Entertainment

Awesome Exploration (182–199)

182-183, Pat Morrow/NGIC; 184 (LE), Marco Grob/NGIC; 184 (RT), Jenny Nichols; 185 (all), Brian Ford; 186-187 (UP), Brian J. Skerry/NGIC; 186 (LO), Brian J. Skerry/NGIC; 187 (CTR), Mark D. Conlin/NGIC; 187 (LO), Brian J. Skerry/NGIC; 188 (background & UP), Paul Nicklen/NGIC; 188 (LO), James C. Chatters; 189 (UP), HI-SEAS/Sian Proctor; 189 (CTR), AP Photo/Hi-Seas; 189 (LO), AP/Rex/SS; 190 (UP RT), Joel Sartore/NGIC; 190 (LO LE), Elliott Ross/NGIC; 190 (LO RT), created by John Gurche/photographed by Mark Thiessen/NGIC; 191 (UP), izusek/GI; 191 (CTR UP), Jim Cumming/GI; 191 (CTR LE), Imgorthand/GI; 191 (CTR CTR), Getman/SS; 191 (CTR RT), Tony Anderson/GI; 192 (both), Ben Arnst/Squaw Valley Alpine Meadows; 193 (UP), Renee Lynn/GI; 193 (LO), Barbara Kinney; 194 (UP LE), Pictures Colour Library/Newscom; 194 (UP RT), Marius Bøstrand; 194 (LO LE), Channi Anand/AP Photo; 194 (LO RT), Bigfoot Hostel/Barcroft Media/GI; 195 (LO LE), Michael Clark/AL; 195 (UP RT), EPA/Newscom; 195 (CTR LE), Anthony Devlin/PA Images/AL; 195 (LO RT), Lucas Jackson/Reuters; 196-197 (all), Annie Griffiths; 198 (UP), Brian J. Skerry/NGIC; 198 (CTR), AP Photo/Hi-Seas; 198 (LO), Bigfoot Hostel/Barcroft Media/GI; 199, Grady Reese/IS

Wonders of Nature (200–219)

200-201, RooM RF/GI; 202 (UP), Manu San Félix; 202 (inset), Rebecca Hale/NG Staff; 203 (all), Enric Sala/NGIC; 205 (UP), Stephanie Sawyer/SS; 205 (LO), Grant Dixon/MP; 206 (UP), Stuart Armstrong; 206 (LO), Franco Tempesta; 207 (UP LE), Leonid Tit/SS; 207 (UP RT), Lars Christensen/SS; 207 (CTR LE), Frans Lanting/NGIC; 207 (CTR RT), Daniel Loretto/SS; 207 (LO), Richard Peterson/SS; 208-209, 3dmotus/SS; 210 (UP), Stephen M. Katz/The Virginian-Pilot via AP; 210 (CTR LE), Carlos Giusti/AP; 210 (CTR RT), Melvin Levongo/AFP/GI; 210 (LO) Australia Broadcasting Corporation via AP; 211 (UP LE), Lori Mehmen/Associated Press; 211 (UP RT & RT CTR), Susan Law Cain/SS; 211 (UP CTR), Brian Nolan/IS; 211 (CTR LE), Judy Kennamer/SS; 211 (LO LE), Jim Reed; 211 (LO CTR & LO RT), jam4travel/SS; 212 (LE), AVTG/IS; 212 (RT), Brad Wynnyk/SS; 213 (UP LE), Rich Carey/SS; 213 (UP RT), Richard Walters/IS; 213 (LO RT), Karen Graham/IS; 213 (LO RT), Michio Hoshino/MP/NGIC; 214-215 (UP), Jason Edwards/NGIC; 214 (LO LE), cbpix/SS; 214 (LO RT), Mike Hill/Photographer's Choice/GI; 215 (LO LE), Wil Meinderts/Buitenbeeld/MP; 215 (LO RT), Paul Nicklen/NGIC; 216-217 (background), John A. Anderson/IS; 216 (UP), Vilainecrevette/SS; 216 (LO), Brandon Cole; 217 (UP), Paul Souders/GI; 217

(LO), Rebecca Hale/NG Staff; 218 (UP), Frans Lanting/NGIC; 218 (CTR), John A. Anderson/IS; 218 (LO), SS

History Happens (220–251)

220-221, Nicola Forenza/IS/GI; 222 (UP), Paul Nicklen/NGIC; 222 (inset), Karla Ortega; 222 (LO), Karla Ortega; 223 (UP), Paul Nicklen/NGIC; 223 (LO), Karla Ortega; 224-225 (background), Pius Lee/SS; 225 (UP LE), Providence Pictures; 225 (UP RT), HOPE PRODUCTIONS/Yann Arthus Bertrand/GI; 225 (LO RT), Hulton Archive/GI; 226 (UP), James L. Stanfield/NGIC; 226 (LO), Photoservice Electa/Universal Images/SuperStock; 227 (all), Joe Rocco; 228, Wang da Gang; 229 (UP LE, UP RT & LO RT), O. Louis Mazzatenta/NGIC; 229 (CTR RT), O. Louis Mazzatenta; 229 (LO LE), Wang da Gang; 230-231 (background), Corey Ford; 230 (LO), Disney Enterprises, Inc./Walden Media, LLC; 231 (UP RT), Ocean/Corbis; 231(LO), Mark Thiessen/NG Staff; 232 (all), Chris Wass; 233 (UP RT), Index Stock Imagery/Jupiterimages/GI; 233 (CTR), Chip Clark/NMNH/Smithsonian Institution; 233 (LO), Superstock, Inc./SuperStock; 234, U.S. Air Force photo/Staff Sgt. Alexandra M. Boutte; 235, Corbis/GI; 236, Scott Rothstein/SS; 237 (UP), AleksandarNakic/IS/GI; 237 (CTR RT), Zack Frank/SS; 237 (LO LE), Gary Blakely/SS; 238 (UP & CTR), AFP/GI; 238 (LO), Education Images/UIG/GI; 239 (all), White House Historical Association; 240 (LO RT), DRMS; 240 (all others), White House Historical Association; 241 (CTR LE), Krissi Lundgren/SS; 241 (all others), White House Historical Association; 242 (LO RT), Francis Miller/Time Life Pictures/GI; 242 (all others), White House Historical Association; 243 (LO CTR RT), lazyllama/SS; 243 (LO RT), Clint Spaulding/WWD/REX/SS; 243 (all others), White House Historical Association; 244-245 (all), Adrian Lubbers; 246 (UP), Bettmann/Corbis/GI; 246 (inset), Science Source/GI; 247 (UP), Charles Kogod/NGIC; 247 (LO LE), iStock Editorial/GI; 247 (LO RT), Chip Somodevilla/GI; 248, Bettmann Archive/GI; 249 (UP LE), Scott Eisen/GI; 249 (UP RT), Mark Wilson/GI; 249 (LO), Bettmann Archive/GI; 250 (UP), Providence Pictures; 250 (CTR), Chris Wass; 250 (LO), Photoservice Electa/Universal Images/SuperStock; 251, Christopher Furlong/GI

Geography Rocks (252–337)

252-253, MelindaChan/GI; 254 (UP), Jon Bowen; 254 (inset), Becky Hale/NG Staff; 255 (UP), International Mapping Inc/NGIC; 255 (LO), Chin Kit Sen/SS; 261 (UP RT), Lori Epstein/NG Staff; 261 (CTR LE), NASA; 262 (background), Fabiano Rebeque/GI; 262 (valley), Thomas J. Abercrombie/NGIC; 262 (river), Maria Stenzel/NGIC; 262 (mountain), Gordon Wiltsie/NGIC; 262 (glacier), James P. Blair/NGIC; 262 (canyon), Bill Hatcher/NGIC; 262 (desert), Carsten Peter/NGIC; 263, f11photo/SS; 264, Amelandfoto/SS; 265 (UP RT), Glowimages/GI; 265 (CTR LE), keyvanchan/GI; 265 (CTR RT), Jean-Jacques Hublin; 265 (LO RT), Dimitri Vervitsiotis/GI; 268, Yva Momatiuk and John Eastcott/MP; 269 (UP RT), Achim Baque/SS; 269 (CTR LE),

Alex Tehrani; 269 (CTR RT), iCreative3D/SS; 269 (LO RT), Aurora Creative/GI; 272, Nguyen Anh Tuan/SS; 273 (UP RT), Jon Arnold Images/Danita Delimont.com; 273 (CTR LE), Ilin Sergey/age fotostock; 273 (CTR RT), Nancy Brown/Photographer's Choice/GI; 273 (LO RT), Daniel Heuclin/NPL/MP; 276, The Image Bank/GI; 277 (UP LE), Mika Stock/Danita Delimont.com; 277 (UP RT), Andrew Watson/John Warburton-Lee Photography Ltd/GI; 277 (CTR RT), FiledIMAGE/SS; 277 (LO), Robert Harding World Imagery/GI; 280, Christian Mueller/SS; 281 (UP RT), Roy Pedersen/SS; 281 (CTR LE), RomarioIen/SS; 281 (CTR RT), Annette Hopf/IS; 281 (LO RT), Mark Gillow/GI; 284, Stone Sub/GI; 285 (UP RT), Rodrigo Arangua/GI; 285 (CTR LE), Gail Shotlander/GI; 285 (CTR RT), Yiming Chen/GI; 285 (LO RT), Janie Blanchard/GI; 288, GI South America/GI; 289 (UP RT), Soberka Richard/hemis.fr/GI; 289 (CTR LE), David Tipling/AL; 289 (CTR RT), DC_Colombia/GI; 289 (LO RT), Walter Diaz/AFP/GI; 295, Maya Karkalicheva/GI; 296, Ondrej Prosicky/SS; 300, Mehmet0/SS; 303, Tim Graham/GI; 304, EyeEm/GI; 308, Bartosz Hadyniak/GI; 311, Peter Cade/GI; 316, Westend61/GI; 328 (UP RT), Panoramic Images/GI; 328 (UP CTR LE), TexPhoto/SS; 328 (UP CTR RT), Harold G Herradura/SS; 328 (LO RT), PhotoDisc; 329 (UP LE), John Warburton Lee/AWL Images; 329 (LO LE), Sumikophoto/DRMS; 329 (RT), Danita Delimont/GI; 330 (UP), Tony McNicol/AL; 330 (CTR), Pioneron/SS; 330-331 (background), Bob Henry/AL; 331 (UP), Walter Bibikow/GI; 331 (CTR LE), Alistair Scott/AL; 331 (LO RT), Stuart Miles/DRMS; 332 (LE), Ilona Ignatova/SS; 332 (CTR LE), Songquan Deng/SS; 332 (CTR), Bokic Bojan/SS; 332 (LO CTR RT), Roman Sigaev/SS; 332 (LO RT), lesapi images/SS; 332 (LO RT), Brian Kinney/SS; 333, Galyna Andrushko/SS; 334 (UP), Shane Talbot/Solent News/REX/SS; 334 (CTR), Mario Armas/Reuters/AL; 334 (LO), ZJAN/Canadian Tire Corporation/WENN/Newscom; 335 (UP), John S Lander/LightRocket/GI; 335 (inset UP), John S Lander/LightRocket/GI; 335 (inset LO), WENN Ltd/AL; 336 (UP), Janie Blanchard/GI; 336 (CTR), Stuart Miles/DRMS; 336 (LO), keyvanchan/GI

Since 1888, the National Geographic Society has funded more than 12,000 research,
exploration, and preservation projects around the world.
The Society receives funds from National Geographic Partners, LLC,
funded in part by your purchase. A portion of the proceeds from this book
supports this vital work. To learn more, visit natgeo.com/info.

NATIONAL GEOGRAPHIC and Yellow Border Design are trademarks of the
National Geographic Society, used under license.

For more information, visit nationalgeographic.com,
call 1-800-647-5463, or write to the following address:

National Geographic Partners
1145 17th Street N.W.
Washington, D.C. 20036-4688 U.S.A.

Visit us online at nationalgeographic.com/books

For librarians and teachers: ngchildrensbooks.org

More for kids from National Geographic: natgeokids.com

National Geographic Kids magazine inspires children to explore their world with fun
yet educational articles on animals, science, nature, and more. Using fresh storytelling and
amazing photography, Nat Geo Kids shows kids ages 6 to 14 the fascinating truth about
the world—and why they should care. **kids.nationalgeographic.com/subscribe**

For information about special discounts for bulk purchases, please contact
National Geographic Books Special Sales: specialsales@natgeo.com

For rights or permissions inquiries, please contact
National Geographic Books Subsidiary Rights: bookrights@natgeo.com

Designed by Kathryn Robbins and Ruthie Thompson

National Geographic supports K–12 educators with ELA Common Core Resources.
Visit natgeoed.org/commoncore for more information.

Trade paperback ISBN: 978-1-4263-3281-4
Hardcover ISBN: 978-1-4263-3282-1

Printed in the United States of America
19/WOR-PCML/1

The publisher would like to thank everyone who worked to make this book come together:
Angela Modany, associate editor; Mary Jones, project editor; Sarah Wassner Flynn,
writer; Michelle Harris, researcher; Lori Epstein, photo director; Hillary Leo, photo editor;
Mike McNey, map production; Stuart Armstrong, illustrator; Sean Philpotts, production
director; Anne LeongSon and Gus Tello, design production assistants;
Sally Abbey, managing editor; Joan Gossett, editorial production manager;
and Alix Inchausti and Molly Reid, production editors.